SERIES-LY CELEBRATING

Book Parties for Popular Children's Series

Sharron Cohen and Christy Rosso

UpstartBooks

Fort Atkinson, Wisconsin

To all the librarians and teachers who get excited about getting others excited about reading.
—S.C.

To my family.
—C.L.R.

Published by UpstartBooks
W5527 State Road 106
P.O. Box 800
Fort Atkinson, Wisconsin 53538-0800
1-800-448-4887

The paper used in this publication meets the minimum requirements of American National Standard for Information Science — Permanence of Paper for Printed Library Material. ANSI/NISO Z39.48-1992.

Table of Contents

Introduction

There are a multitude of books and Web sites devoted to the use of children's literature in reinforcing curriculum. *Series-ly Celebrating* has a somewhat different purpose. The book is written for librarians who want centerpiece activities for reading promotion programs and for teachers who want to finish their classroom literature units with an event that can lure parents, grandparents, and siblings into the school. It is a book about celebrating literature with a baker's dozen of the series that are currently most popular with young readers.

We've suggested a variety of events, weaving our suggestions around the elements in the books we think please, intrigue, amuse, and touch readers. In some cases, we've suggested ways to make those events more or less complex. But we've never lost sight of the fact that these programs are supposed to be celebratory. That's why we've devoted a lot of space to ideas for appropriate refreshments and the kinds of games and activities that will interest children of all ages. Some of our recipes and crafts contain nuts or peanut butter. We recommend that you consider potential food allergies in planning your activity or event.

The projects in this book require planning and effort. We are advocates of the "many hands" theory of life. We believe in asking parents, volunteers, former teachers, nice people in the neighborhood, and most especially, young people themselves to pitch in at all levels of planning, execution, and cleanup. We also encourage tailoring our suggestions to the needs and interests of your particular community.

We hope you have fun with the events we offer in these pages.

Amelia Bedelia

Authors: Peggy Parish and Herman Parish • **Illustrators:** Fritz Siebel, Barbara Siebel Thomas, Wallace Tripp, Lynn Sweat • **Publisher:** HarperCollins
Age Level: 6–8 years old

Amelia Bedelia is a housekeeper whose literal-minded behaviors cause constant chaos in the Rogers household. Only her ability to cook redeems the situation and keeps her gainfully employed. This early reader series is popular among students who, beginning to negotiate the vagaries of the English language themselves, are amused by Amelia Bedelia's constant misunderstanding of homonyms and idioms.

Amelia Bedelia's abilities in the kitchen make her a predecessor of Martha Stewart. It's time to declare Amelia Bedelia the original "Domestic Diva" and invoke her spirit in one of America's favorite activities—the Scrapbook Party.

Amelia Bedelia Scrapbook Party

Asked to create a scrapbook, Amelia Bedelia would probably create a book of cloth scraps or stitch together scraps of other books. We suggest you not be quite that literal. Bring together participants (students alone or students with adults) to make scrapbooks in the homonym- and idiom-challenged style of Amelia Bedelia.

You will need:

- a scrapbook for every child (**Note:** You can also make your own, see pages 8–9.)

- paper (construction, colored, or white drawing paper)

- pencils, colored markers, pens, crayons, glitter glue

- decorative elements (bits of lace, wallpaper, metallic paper, food labels)

- pictures, words, and letters cut from glossy magazines (Ask volunteers to help you do this in advance to save time.)

- scissors

- white glue and glue sticks

- pre-made labels—Make them on a computer, or use a copy machine to replicate labels you have made by hand. Label possibilities include:

I am …

I like to do these things

This is my family

This is where I live

These are my friends

These are my teachers

I do these things at home

I do these things at school

My hobbies are …

When I grow up I want to be …

The foods I like… The foods I dislike…

- blank dialogue balloons of varied sizes

- photographs of every participant

Helpful hints:

- Every child should have at least one photo of him- or herself in the book. Ensure the highest degree of success by asking parents well in advance to collect photos of their children, especially outtake photos they won't mind seeing cut up. Follow up with frequent reminders in notes home, on the school's Web site, and in the school's newsletter.

- Consider enlisting volunteers with digital cameras to photograph everyone in the class engaged in the kind of activities that would be useful for the scrapbooks. Encourage participants to think like Amelia Bedelia (for example, making a sponge cake out of sponges). Have students look over the list of homonyms and idioms on pages 11–13 so they can bring in props to stage photographs. Print the photos out (paper copies of the photos are adequate) and make them available on the day of the party.

- Create a sample scrapbook that can be displayed before and during the scrapbook party. Combine photos, drawings, words, and pictures cut from magazines, titles, captions, dialogue balloons, arrows, stars, exclamation and question marks, and decorative borders. Employ a wide variety of techniques in order to show participants the possibilities for their own projects.

- Make copies of the homonyms and idioms list for every participant, or post the list where participants can refer to it.

- This is a great activity in which to include grandparents. If you decide to invite grandparents, it might be a good idea to create a pool of "extras" (retired teachers, parents of teachers and librarians, older neighbors) for students who do not have grandparents able to participate. Arrange for any volunteers to borrow at least one book from the Amelia Bedelia series in order to familiarize themselves with Amelia Bedelia's quirky literalness.

Creating Scrapbooks

If a scrapbook for each child is too expensive for your classroom or library budget, you can make less expensive scrapbooks. Decide ahead of time which style you will be creating; you may choose to have volunteers help you create the scrapbooks.

Three-ring Binder Scrapbooks

Obtain three-ring binders (either soft or hardcover varieties) and packages of clear plastic sheet protectors. (Make sure the sheet protectors are the three-hole punch variety, compatible with the three-ring binders.) Have participants work on 8½" x 11" colored or white copy paper or construction paper. (**Note:** Construction paper, which is often 9" x 12", may require trimming to fit into an 8½" x 11" sheet protector.) When the page has been assembled, slip it into the sheet protector. When a second page has been assembled, slide it into the same sheet protector, with the backs of the pages together. Fold a piece of transparent tape over the opening of the sheet protector. Assemble the rest of the pages in the same way, then put them in order and insert them in the binder. Students can decorate the cover with glitter glue, photos, or other decorative elements.

Scrapbooks with Poster Board Covers

Cut 2 pieces of 10" x 13" white or colored poster board (per scrapbook). The pieces will make a cover that is ½" larger than the scrapbook pages on the left-hand edge, and 1" larger on the top, bottom, and right-hand edges. Use a ruler to draw a line ½" from the edge of one of the long (13") sides. Press the curved end of a paper clip against the ruler and run it firmly along the line, then bend the poster along that line. Do the same on the second piece of poster board. This helps the covers open more easily when the scrapbook is assembled. Place the two pieces of poster board

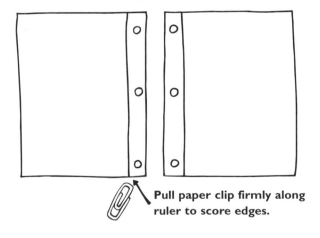

Pull paper clip firmly along ruler to score edges.

together so that the covers bend away from each other. Using one of the sheet protectors as a template, punch three matching holes in each piece of poster board. Create the scrapbook pages in the manner described for the three-ring binder scrapbook. Assemble them, sandwich them between the poster board covers, and slide brads through the holes. Have participants decorate the covers with markers, glitter glue, and photos.

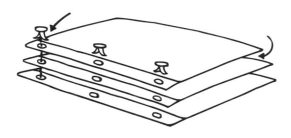

Cloth-covered Scrapbooks

Fancier scrapbook covers can be made of cloth-covered poster board or cardboard. Follow the directions for poster board covers described above. Cut two pieces of 10" x 13" cloth. Glue a cloth piece to each cover—these will be the insides of the covers. Cut two more pieces of cloth an inch larger all around (12" x 15") and glue those pieces to the outer sides of the covers. Cut a "V" shape at each corner, fold the material around the corner and glue the edges along the inside of the cover. Use an awl to punch holes for brass fasteners as in the poster board directions. Because this is a difficult process for young students, and their use of an awl is inadvisable, cloth-covered scrapbooks should be created by adult volunteers. Students can select the cloth to use and decorate the finished cover with glitter glue.

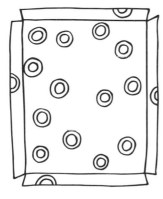
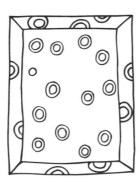

Creating the Scrapbook Pages

On the day of the Amelia Bedelia Scrapbook Party, lay an array of materials out on a central table and place the sample scrapbook where it will be available for inspiration. Give every participant (or team of participants, if students and adults are working together) a scrapbook (or materials to make one), paper, scissors, glue, crayons, markers, student photos, and lists of homonyms and idioms. Invite scrapbook makers to take materials from the central table as needed.

Get the activity started by suggesting that participants use the pre-made labels, at least for the first few pages. For instance, a scrapbook could start with "I AM" at the top of the first page, with a photo of the student beneath it and a dialogue balloon in which he or she writes his or her name or the word "Hello." Another page could start with the label "I LIKE TO" above a picture of a fish and the word "fish" cut out of magazine text, followed by the label "I DON'T LIKE" with a photo of the child scrubbing a fish with a scrub brush and the words "to," "clean," and "them." If no idiom photos were staged before the scrapbook party, the page could combine magazine photos of a fish and a scrub brush or bucket.

Refreshments

Amelia Bedelia Scrapbook Party participants could all get a piece of sponge cake and a good punch, but Amelia Bedelia would be appalled at the idea of hitting guests. The housekeeper's specialties are strawberry tarts and pie, especially lemon meringue and apple. Tea would be appropriate for the adults in the room. Strawberry-flavored juice or punch would be appropriate for the children. Make sure the refreshments come at the end of the activity, lest the scrapbooks become jammed with more than memories.

Web Sites

The Series and Authors

Amelia Bedelia in the Classroom: Terryville Second Grade Students Present Amelia Bedelia
comsewogue.k12.ny.us/~csinger/projects/amelia/amelia.htm
An appealing elementary school Web site that showcases word problems, activities, and student work with some of the idioms found in the Amelia Bedelia series.

Harper Collins, Amelia Bedelia
www.harperchildrens.com/hch/fiction/featuresarchive/amelia/index.asp
The publisher's Web site contains word games and coloring sheets.

Herman Parish, AuthorTracker, HarperCollins
www.authortracker.com/author.asp?a=authorid&b=17963
Author bio and book list.

KidsReads.com
www.kidsreads.com/series/series-amelia-titles.asp
Book list, author bio, trivia game, fast facts.

Welcome to Mrs. Gray's Classroom
www.genevaschools.org/austinbg/class/gray/writers/amelia.htm
Results of a class project in which students wrote about their substitute teacher, Amelia Bedelia.

Scrapbooks

Make Mini Scrapbooks from Ziploc Bags
ut.essortment.com/makeminiscrapb_pzw.htm
Inexpensive scrapbook ideas.

Books in the Amelia Bedelia Series

Amelia Bedelia books by Peggy Parish

Amelia Bedelia illustrated by Fritz Siebel

Thank You, Amelia Bedelia illustrated by Barbara Siebel Thomas

Amelia Bedelia and the Surprise Shower illustrated by Barbara Siebel Thomas

Come Back, Amelia Bedelia illustrated by Wallace Tripp

Play Ball, Amelia Bedelia illustrated by Wallace Tripp

Good Work, Amelia Bedelia illustrated by Lynn Sweat

Teach Us, Amelia Bedelia illustrated by Lynn Sweat

Amelia Bedelia Helps Out illustrated by Lynn Sweat

Amelia Bedelia and the Baby illustrated by Lynn Sweat

Amelia Bedelia Goes Camping illustrated by Lynn Sweat

Merry Christmas, Amelia Bedelia illustrated by Lynn Sweat

Amelia Bedelia's Family Album illustrated by Lynn Sweat

Amelia Bedelia books by Herman Parish

Good Driving, Amelia Bedelia illustrated by Lynn Sweat

Bravo, Amelia Bedelia! illustrated by Lynn Sweat

Amelia Bedelia 4 Mayor illustrated by Lynn Sweat

Calling Doctor Amelia Bedelia illustrated by Lynn Sweat

Amelia Bedelia and the Christmas List illustrated by Lynn Sweat

Amelia Bedelia, Bookworm illustrated by Lynn Sweat

Amelia Bedelia Goes Back to School illustrated by Lynn Sweat

Be My Valentine, Amelia Bedelia illustrated by Lynn Sweat

Amelia Bedelia, Rocket Scientist? illustrated by Lynn Sweat

Amelia Bedelia Under Construction illustrated by Lynn Sweat

Happy Haunting, Amelia Bedelia illustrated by Lynn Sweat

Homonyms and Idioms

Around the House and Yard

- Change the towels in the bathroom. (*Amelia Bedelia cuts them up.*)
- Dust the furniture. (*She uses dusting powder.*)
- Draw the drapes. (*She sketches them.*)
- Put the lights out. (*She hangs them on a clothes-line.*)
- Strip the sheets. (*She tears them into strips.*)
- Check the shirts when they come back from the laundry. (*She puts checks on them.*)
- Run over the tablecloth with an iron. (*She runs across it holding an iron.*)
- Put cut flowers in a bowl. (*She cuts the flowers into pieces.*)
- Pot the window box plants. (*She puts them in kitchen pots.*)
- Patch the screen. (*She uses a cloth patch.*)
- Stuff Christmas stockings. (*She uses chicken stuffing.*)
- Trim the tree. (*She uses clippers to shorten the branches of the tree.*)
- Put colored balls on the tree. (*She uses children's balls.*)
- String on lights. (*She puts string on the lights.*)
- Prune the hedge. (*She decorates the hedge with prunes.*)
- Weed the garden. (*She adds weeds.*)
- Stake the beans. (*She puts a steak on each plant.*)
- Dust for potato bugs. (*She uses dusting powder.*)
- Throw scraps to chickens. (*She uses cloth scraps.*)
- Sow the grass seeds. (*She sews them together.*)

In the Kitchen

- Make pancakes. (*Amelia Bedelia makes cakes in a frying pan.*)
- Measure two cups of rice. (*She measures them with a ruler.*)
- Trim the fat before putting steaks into the icebox. (*She decorates the steaks.*)
- Dress the chicken. (*She puts clothes on it.*)
- Fix a chicken dinner. (*She fixes a cracked corn dinner for a chicken.*)
- String the beans. (*She puts them on a string.*)
- Make jelly roll. (*She rolls jelly on the counter.*)
- Separate three eggs. (*She puts them elsewhere.*)
- Pare vegetables. (*She places the vegetables in pairs.*)
- Scale the fish. (*She weighs it.*)
- Ice the fish. (*She covers it with frosting.*)
- Make a tea cake. (*She puts tea in the cake.*)
- Give me cereal with my morning coffee. (*She puts cereal in the coffee.*)
- Put on a can of soup. (*She wears a can of soup.*)
- Make chocolate chip cookies. (*She makes chocolate cookies with potato chips.*)
- Put dates in the cake. (*She cuts dates from the calendar.*)
- Make a sponge cake. (*She uses sponges.*)
- Give a surprise shower. (*She squirts party guests with a hose.*)

Vacation and Travel

- Pick him up at the train. (*She tried but he was too heavy.*)
- Catch a train. (*She thinks it takes two hands because it's heavy.*)
- Jump in the car. (*While inside the car, she jumps.*)
- Hit the road. (*She hits it.*)
- Pitch the tent. (*She tosses it.*)
- Row the boats. (*She lines them up.*)
- Cut tent stakes. (*She cuts steaks to look like tents.*)
- Go fly a kite. (*Meant as "go away"; she gets a kite and flies it.*)
- Herd of cows. (*She has heard of cows.*)
- Push on the horn. (*She pushes on a cow's horn.*)

- Would you like me to give you a tow? (*She already has ten toes.*)
- Get directions. (*She returns with road signs.*)
- Look for the fork in the road. (*She looks for silverware in the middle of the road.*)
- Bear left. (*She thinks the animal went that direction.*)
- Left is right. (*Meant as "correct"; she thinks her right hand is her left hand, and vice versa.*)
- There is a crossroad. (*She thinks the road is angry.*)

Playing Baseball

- Warm up. (*Amelia Bedelia puts on a winter coat.*)
- Tag Jack. (*She puts a clothing tag on him.*)
- Wear a uniform. (*She comes to a baseball game in a military uniform.*)
- Put Dick out. (*She carries Dick off the field.*)
- Steal second base and run home. (*She steals the base and runs home with it.*)
- Keep score. (*She offers to keep it in a locked chest.*)
- Home plate. (*She puts cookies on it.*)

At School

- Call the roll. (*Amelia Bedelia calls to a student's lunch roll.*)
- Plant bulbs. (*She puts light bulbs into pots.*)
- Paint pictures. (*She paints over other pictures.*)
- It's time for play practice. (*She practices playing games.*)

In Music Class

- Practice a few numbers. (*Amelia Bedelia practices numerals.*)
- Tap your toe. (*She taps her toe with her finger.*)
- B flat. (*She lays flat on the floor.*)
- Read notes. (*She reads only notes addressed to her.*)
- Play by ear. (*She plays beside her ear.*)
- Play it lower. (*She sits on the floor.*)

- Wind instrument. (*An electric fan.*)
- Horns. (*On a Viking hat.*)
- Triangle. (*A piece of paper shaped like a triangle.*)
- String instrument. (*A piece of string.*)
- Use a violin bow. (*She also uses barrettes and ribbons.*)
- Drum roll. (*The drum rolls across the floor.*)

At the Library

- Books need jackets. (*Amelia Bedelia makes them coats.*)
- I want to hear a pin drop. (*She drops pins.*)
- Go by the book. (*She buys a book.*)
- Take the Bookmobile. (*"Take" meant as "for example."*)
- Throw the book at you. (*Said by a policeman.*)
- Bookmobile (*A child makes Amelia Bedelia a bookmobile mobile.*)

Babysitting

- Give the baby a bottle. (*Amelia Bedelia gives the baby a can and box instead.*)
- Use baby powder. (*She uses it on herself.*)
- Don't forget nap time. (*She thinks the order is for her to nap.*)
- Give the baby a mashed banana. (*She mashes the entire banana, including the peel.*)
- Put the baby in the stroller and take her out. (*She puts the baby in the stroller and takes her out again.*)
- Put on Missy's bib. (*She puts it on herself.*)
- Give her baby food. (*She makes tiny hamburgers, potatoes, and tomatoes.*)

Occupations

- At the Doctor's Office—Putting on the doctor's gloves. (*Amelia Bedelia puts them on herself.*)
- At the Beauty Shop—Pinning up a woman's hair. (*She uses safety pins.*)
- At the Dress Shop—Shortening dresses. (*She cuts them off with scissors.*)

- In an Office—Stamping envelopes. (*She jumps on them.*) Filing papers. (*She uses a fingernail file.*)

Jobs Held by Amelia Bedelia's Family Members

- Daddy is a telephone operator. (*He operates on phones.*)
- Mama is a loafer. (*She makes bread.*)
- Uncle Albert is a big game hunter. (*He searches for large-size games.*)
- Aunt Mary is a bank teller. (*She tells people which bank to use.*)
- Cousin Calvin is a boxer. (*He packs boxes.*)
- Cousin Edward is a horse racer. (*He runs along beside horses.*)
- Uncle Ned is a Cook. (*That's his name.*)
- Uncle Dan takes pictures. (*He's a thief.*)
- Cousin Bea balances checkbooks. (*She can balance twenty at a time while standing on one foot.*)
- Brother Ike wants an orange grove. (*But all the trees he orders turn out green.*)
- Cousin Chester is a printer. (*He never learned proper writing.*)
- Cousin Clara is a bookkeeper. (*She never gives them back.*)
- Cousin Ella works with Clay. (*Her husband.*)
- Uncle Alf collects garbage. (*He keeps it in his yard.*)
- Cousin Susan belongs to a fan club. (*She collects fans.*)
- Niece Lulu stuffs olives. (*She stuffs them into herself.*)
- Nephew Ollie is a catcher. (*He catches measles, mumps, and colds.*)

Politics

- Run for office. (*Amelia Bedelia runs to the Mayor's office.*)
- We need a change. (*She offers 43 cents.*)
- I want to put in my two cents. (*She gives two pennies.*)
- The mayor doesn't have any sense. (*She thinks he is out of change, "cents."*)
- Take a poll. (*She thinks she needs a pole.*)
- Most voters are sitting on the fence. (*She thinks people are sitting on fences.*)
- We're going to the White House. (*Amelia Bedelia goes to see Mrs. White.*)

Additional Idioms

- On your toes.
- Knock it off.
- Hop to it.
- Grit your teeth.
- The word is on the tip of my tongue.
- Shake a leg.
- Keep your eyes on the board (*or on me*).
- Hold your tongue, bite your tongue, cat got your tongue.
- He went ape, she went bananas, I was nuts.
- Rise and shine.
- Hold your horses.
- Frog in my throat.
- Spit it out. (*Meaning "Say it."*)
- Caught a bug.
- Something's fishy.
- On thin ice.
- Eyes in the back of her head.
- He's a dear (deer).
- Eats like a bird, eats like a horse, eats like a pig.
- Feeling blue, seeing red, in the pink.
- Spilled the beans.
- Apple of his eye.
- Clean a fish.
- Run a bulldozer.

Magic Tree House

Author: Mary Pope Osborne • **Illustrator:** Sal Murdocca
Publisher: Random House • **Age Level:** 6–8 years old

In the more than thirty volumes of the Magic Tree House series, siblings Jack and Annie time-travel with the help of a magic tree house. The adventures, which usually involve a narrow escape from dangers such as pirates, volcanic eruptions, sinking ships, and lions, serve the purpose of placing the children in different moments in history. One thread that binds the series together is the presence of Morgan Le Fay and Merlin the Wizard. The two mythical characters send the children on tasks that range from breaking spells and collecting books for preservation, to learning life lessons such as Be Wise, Be Brave, and Be Careful, or Find Magic in Everyday Life.

The books are augmented by an excellent series of nonfiction Magic Tree House Research Guides, cowritten by Mary Pope Osborne and her husband Will Osborne, or her sister Natalie Pope Boyce. Every book in the companion series includes a section that gives advice on doing research, recommendations for books, videos, CD-ROMs and Web sites, and suggestions for activities at zoos and museums.

Magic Tree House Exposition

There are numerous ways to use the Magic Tree House series to reinforce history, geography, and language arts lessons in the classroom. (The Web site section of this chapter lists several Web sites with applicable lesson plans.) Our celebration of the series focuses on the heart of the stories—the tree house itself. Plan a Magic Tree House Exposition, where participants can showcase their wildest imaginings for tree houses of all kinds through design drawings, scale models, or even edible versions. Groups could work together to design an entire tree house town that includes homes, schools, restaurants, and libraries. Invite adults to submit designs as well, or encourage families to create ideas together.

Planning Your Magic Tree House Exposition

The Magic Tree House Exposition can encompass a variety of tree house-related exhibits, including designs of fantasy tree houses, models of fairy tree houses and bird tree houses, edible tree houses, and leaf rubbings. Some projects, like the fantasy tree house designs, can be prepared by participants at home and submitted for exhibition. Some activities, like creating individual edible tree houses, can be conducted at a crafts table during the exposition. However, a number of the activities in this chapter can be created at workshops held prior to the exposition. The products of the workshops can then be displayed at the Magic Tree House Exposition. Read through this entire chapter thoroughly to plan how to set up your exposition.

Fantasy Tree Houses

Invite participants to submit designs for their wildest dream/fantasy tree houses. Younger students can draw pictures. Older participants can provide more detailed plans showing the tree house from several angles, with floor plans that note stairs, elevators, and other important features. Have participants prepare designs in advance for display at the exposition. Encourage them to seek help from family members or other adults.

Fairy Tree Houses

Building human-sized tree houses with the participants in your Magic Tree House Exposition might be impractical, but everyone can build a tree house if the scale of the project is reduced. Consider holding workshops to build tree houses for fairies and other winged creatures. The houses can even be placed in trees after being displayed at the exposition.

Cathedral Woods on Monhegan Island, Maine, is filled with fairy houses—twig and leaf creations built by humans to encourage fairy habitation. The fairies in your neighborhood have no less need of housing and, since they can fly, they would probably enjoy tree house versions of those dwellings.

Fairy House

Start by arranging a field trip to the woods or to a park to collect materials, or ask students to bring natural materials from home. Materials can include twigs, dried stalks, cornhusks, leaves and vines (for hammocks), acorns, pinecones and nuts (for furniture), and silver dollar pods (for shingles and windows). Materials should be found on the ground, not stripped from living plants. Though less authentic, craft sticks and cardboard can also be used, especially if the fairy houses are not going to be placed in the woods. If the fairy houses are to be left in the woods, care should be taken not to use materials that will create unsightly litter when the houses disintegrate.

Provide white glue, natural fiber yarns, and string. Assist participants in assembling their materials. Add a string loop to the top of the fairy house so it can hang from a limb. Fairy tree houses need not be substantial. They can be as fragile and whimsical as the fairy folk themselves.

After the fairy houses are exhibited at the Magic Tree House Exposition, accompany participants to the placement site and assist them in hanging the fairy houses from tree limbs or nestling them into the crooks of trees. Participants could also take their fairy tree houses home for their own gardens, or the tree houses could find a home in the school or library's potted plants.

Bird Tree Houses

Maybe fairies do not exist (we are reserving judgment on the matter), but there are other winged creatures who appreciate tree houses as much as fairies do. Hold a workshop, or series of workshops, to construct birdhouses.

Birdhouses from Kits

Sometimes the easiest way for children to make a satisfying birdhouse is to use a kit. Check local bird supply stores, Audubon Society chapters, department stores, or online for the price of birdhouses purchased in quantity.

Gourd Birdhouses

Provide each participant with a dried bottle gourd (sometimes called a birdhouse gourd). Drill or cut a hole in the upper half of the gourd. A 1½" diameter hole is a good size, but check the Gourd Birdhouses Web site (see page 21) if you want to match the size of the opening with a specific species of bird. Use a stick or long-handled teaspoon to clean out as many seeds as possible. Drill a few small holes in the bottom of the gourd for drainage. Wipe the outside of the gourd with a cloth dampened with water and vinegar to remove dirt and mold. After the gourd is dry, shellac it for preservation. To hang the gourd birdhouse, attach a wire through the base of the stem.

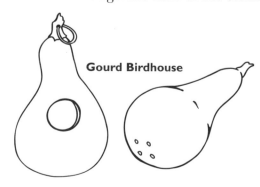

Gourd Birdhouse

Nests

Encourage participants to create nests using dried grasses, leaves, and yarn. A messier version could include mud or clay softened with water, formed in plastic or paper bowls and allowed to dry. Exhibit the nests at the Magic Tree House Exposition, then place them in crooks of trees.

Edible Tree Houses

Set up a craft table where participants can make graham cracker and pretzel tree houses. The finished products can be exhibited or eaten.

Graham Cracker Tree House

Provide plain or chocolate-covered graham crackers, a tube of icing, and a stiff paper or plastic plate for each participant. Stand two graham crackers on end and cement their edges with icing. Add two more graham crackers in the same way until you have a graham cracker square. Pipe icing along the top edges and carefully lay a fifth graham cracker across the top as a roof. Add decorations by using the icing to glue on licorice sticks, candy buttons, pretzels, gum drops, tic-tacs, and other candies.

A somewhat more stable way to construct the edible tree house is to use an 8-ounce, washed milk carton with the top removed. Use icing or smooth peanut butter to glue a graham cracker to each side. Lay a graham cracker across the top. Decorate as described above.

Pretzel Tree House

Start with a brownie or bar cookie base. Stick thin pretzels into the brownie ¼" inside its edges. (Do not push the pretzels all the way through the brownie.) Lay a cookie or graham cracker across the top of the pretzel posts. Decorate with icing and a licorice rope.

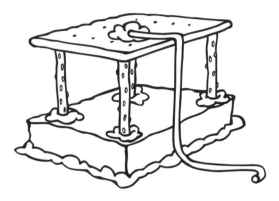

Ground-level Tree Houses

Creating ground-level tree houses in the exposition hall is not only a fun project to do with participants, it's also a great way to decorate the hall. Choose between the following materials:

Large Appliance Box

Set the box on its side. Create a door by cutting three sides of a rectangle and adding a cabinet knob for a doorknob, or cut the door away completely. Cut away squares for windows or cut a sideways "H" and fold back the flaps for shutters. The box could be cut but otherwise left undecorated until the day of the Magic Tree House Exposition, when participants could paint and decorate the box to resemble a tree house, right down to leaves, birds, squirrels, and window box planters. Provide markers, paper leaves, and any other decorations you can think of.

Appliance Box Tree House

Folding Cardboard Display Boards

Available in 36" x 48" sizes in office supply stores, these boards can be moved around to create a small tree house area for individual or small group activities or expanded outward to accommodate a larger group. Invite participants to create paper flower and leaf garlands to decorate the tree house. Participants can also create drawings of their favorite Magic Tree House locales, which could be hung as window scenes on the inside of the display panel tree house.

Folding Cardboard Display

Newspapers

More complicated and permanent than the previous two ground-level tree houses, the newspaper log cabin could be used for other classroom or library activities, such as units focusing on pioneer life or historical fiction. We recommend that the cabin be framed prior to log building with 2" x 4" studs for stability if the cabin is to be used by children.

Newspaper Log Cabin

Materials:

- newspapers (25" x 22" sheets)
- newspaper circulars (17" x 10" sheets)
- 15-ounce cans, empty and clean
- large piece of heavy cardboard
- burlap
- masking tape
- brown craft paper
- brown packaging tape
- heavy twine
- glue gun
- awl or screwdriver

Before You Begin:

- Collect newspapers, newspaper circulars, and 15-ounce cans.

- Each long log requires 60 sheets of newspaper and six 15-ounce cans. Each short log requires six advertising circulars and two 15-ounce cans.

- A windowless log cabin requires 31 long logs. (Eight logs each for the two side walls, seven logs for the back wall, and eight corner post logs. The fourth side of the cabin is left open to serve as a door.) Fourteen short logs are needed (seven for each side of the door opening).

- A log cabin with a window requires 28 long logs and 20 short logs. (Six short logs will replace three long logs on the back wall.)

Construct Long Logs and Short Logs:

1. Lay two newspaper sheets horizontally, side-by-side, with a 2" overlap between the sheets. Place two newspaper sheets on top of the first two sheets, positioned vertically.

2. Layer the sheets until you have ten layers; tape the edges together.

3. Repeat two more times, until you have thirty layers. Tape all of the layers together.

4. Tape two cans together with masking tape, open ends facing. Use six cans per log, posi-

tioning the double cans at each end and in the middle of the log. Fix the newspaper to the cans with a strip of masking tape.

5. Roll the log up tightly. (This is a two-person job.) Wrap a liberal amount of masking tape around the newspaper log.

6. For a finished look, wrap the logs in brown craft paper and seal with brown packing tape.

7. Use the same method for creating the short logs, but use a single can at each end of the log.

Create the Cabin:

1. Stack the logs like toy Lincoln Logs to create a structure with three walls. (The fourth side will be a large door.) Start by laying down the two side walls.

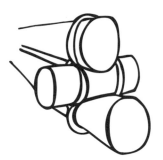

2. Place a long log across the back, resting on the side wall logs with a few inches of overlap at each end.

3. Place a short log at a right angle to the long log at each of the front corners (where the door will be). Use a glue gun to glue the logs together at the corners of the cabin.

4. Continue until the cabin is eight logs high on the sides and seven logs high in the back.

5. When the walls are completed, place the corner posts inside the house and use twine to tie them in place in the corners, winding the twine in a figure eight around the corner post and building logs.

6. Place four more logs in the four corners outside the cabin and tie them in place in the same manner.

7. To build a window into the back wall of the cabin, build the structure as described for four layers of long logs on the back wall. Then use the short logs, placed at right angles to the long logs of the side walls, at the two back corners of the cabin. (The window will be the width of the entire back wall.) Continue using the short logs instead of the long logs for the remainder of the back wall. Fix the eight corner posts in place as described above.

8. To make a flat roof, glue a piece of burlap to a large piece of cardboard so that the burlap slightly overlaps the edges. Weave twine through the burlap, then tie it to the twine at the corner posts.

9. To make a peaked roof, obtain a large appliance box and cut away the top and bottom flaps and two of the sides. Use an awl or screwdriver to make holes in the corners of the cardboard. Loop twine through the holes and around the newspaper logs.

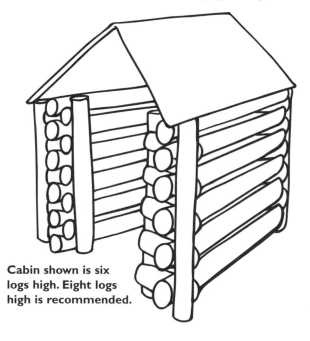

Cabin shown is six logs high. Eight logs high is recommended.

Decorating with Leaves

Use the following methods to create leaves for decorating the ground-level tree houses, or combine the leaves into garlands and transform the entire room into a tree house.

Leaf Rubbings

Collect a variety of leaves and place them on a table. Lay construction paper over the leaves and rub the paper with the side of a crayon (paper wrapper removed) to create a textured leaf pattern. Display the leaf rubbings as they are arranged on the paper or cut the leaves out and staple them to green or brown ribbon, crepe paper streamers, or gathered swags of lightweight fabric.

Pressed Leaves

Collect a variety of leaves. Lay them flat between two sheets of waxed paper and place several heavy books on top of them. After a few days, remove the books and discard the wax paper. Lay each leaf on a piece of clear contact paper (sticky side up) and cover with another piece of clear contact paper. Cut around the leaf. Staple the leaf to a ribbon or crepe paper streamer, tape it to a tree branch, or use a paper punch to create a hole and add a loop of string for hanging.

Refreshments

A larger version of the edible tree house can serve as the centerpiece on the refreshment table. Get creative with your refreshments using the ideas below:

Magic Tree House Cake

Prepare any cake mix according to the package instructions. Pour the batter into a clean, greased, and floured 2-pound metal coffee can. Bake for approximately 55 minutes or until a cake tester inserted into the middle of the cake comes out clean. Loosen the cake around its edges with a spatula, turn the can over, and gently remove the cake. Cool upright on a wire rack. The cake can be used in its round form, or it can be trimmed with a sharp, serrated knife to make it a more traditional rectangle.

Frost the cake with chocolate or mocha icing. Use a contrasting color of icing to make vertical lines that look like boards. Make trees with black licorice or breadstick trunks and green mint candy leaves (cut them crosswise to make them thinner and lighter). Use candy wafers for windows and squares of chocolate candy bars for a door. For a bird's nest, melt choco-late chips in a microwave oven, mix with chow mein noodles, and form into a nest. Fill with candy eggs or jelly beans, glued down with a dab of icing. Add a marshmallow bird and a gummy worm inchworm if desired. Place the cake on an elevated cake stand and hang a licorice rope over the edge of the stand.

Cupcakes

Frost cupcakes to look like smaller tree houses, arrange them amid celery trees on a cake stand, and hang licorice ropes over the edge of the plate.

Vegetable Forest

Create a forest of vegetable crudités by standing leafy celery stalks upright in glasses or mugs. Create a dip landscape by putting one inch of spinach or other green dip into a glass pie pan. Cut broccoli florets with an inch and a half of stem and slightly longer celery stalks with leaves. Arrange the vegetables to look like bushes around the edges of the dip pond.

Tree House Snack

Cut a lettuce leaf to look like a maple, oak, or other leaf. Shape soft cheddar cheese spread into a tree house shape. Roll the cheese in chopped nuts (optional). Set it on the lettuce leaf. Decorate it to look like a tree house, using zucchini shingles for the roof and red or green pepper squares for windows and doors. Serve with crackers.

Leafy Green Punch

Serve limeade or limeade combined with equal amounts of ginger ale or tonic water. Float a leafy-branch-with-cherries ice ring in the punch to keep it cool.

To make the ice ring, soak a short, supple leafy branch in a bowl of water to remove any insect life. Bend it into a circle the size of a gelatin mold or bundt pan and keep it in position with a twist tie. Arrange cherries around the bottom of the pan. Place the branch, leaves facing down, on top of the cherries. Pour in just enough ginger ale or limeade to cover the cherries and branch. Freeze. When the branch has frozen in place, add enough liquid to bring the mold to the desired depth. Return to the freezer until ready to unmold.

Other Displays

An exposition benefits from having a wide variety of displays and activities. If you have room, consider adding the following:

Student Work

If students did classroom work related to the Magic Tree House series, mount and display it for the exposition.

Magic Tree House Popularity Award

Ask guests to vote for their favorite Magic Tree House book. Post a list of the books to jog readers' memories.

Magic Tree House Travel Agency

Ask guests to vote on the place and time they would most like to visit if they had access to a magic time-traveling tree house. Announce the most popular answers at the end of the exposition or later in the school or library newsletter or on the Web site.

Test Your Tree IQ

Mount a tree display. At its simplest, the display could include leaves or photos of leaves. Ask players to identify the trees from which the leaves came. Make the game easier by posting a list of possible answers. The game could be made more complicated by adding fruits and nuts and asking participants to match them to the correct leaves. Post or announce the correct answers at the end of the exposition.

Tree Houses Around the World

Recruit a group of participants to research and create an exhibit of actual tree houses around the world.

Guest Exhibitors

Ask local experts to mount exhibits or information tables at the exposition. Possibilities include travel agents (with tree house destinations), Audubon Society and bird-watching experts (to talk about birdhouses), and arborists (to talk about constructing tree houses without injuring trees).

Games

Magic Tree House Relay Race

Premise of the game: Merlin is under a spell that Morgan Le Fay can break if she is given objects in the correct order. The first team of players to give her all the objects wins the game.

Set-up: Divide players into two equal teams. Players line up at one end of the room. Place a wizard hat for each team at the opposite side of the room, with Morgan Le Fay standing between them. The hats should contain an identical assortment of small items, such as a key, spoon, toy car, acorn, pencil, etc.

Play: Morgan Le Fay announces the first item she needs. The first player in each team's line goes to his or her team's hat, finds the item, and gives it to Morgan Le Fay. She tells that team member what the next item is. The team member returns to his or her team and tells the next person in line which item to select from the hat. Play continues until all of the items in one team's hat have been given to Morgan Le Fay.

Magic Tree House Elimination

Decorate squares of cardboard to represent the locations of books in the Magic Tree House series. (This can be done earlier by children at a crafts table, though they should be told their drawings will be stepped on.) Set the cardboard squares in a circle and instruct players to walk around them while music is played. When the music stops, players need to step on a tree house. (Only one player can occupy a tree house at a time.) For the next round, a tree house is eliminated. The player who is not standing on a tree house when the music stops is eliminated. Then another tree house is removed. Play continues, with one tree house eliminated every round, until there are two students left and only one tree house. The player who is standing on that tree house when the music stops is the winner.

Web Sites

The Series and Author

Book Units from the Magic Tree House Series
www.mce.k12tn.net/units/tree_house.htm
A book by book, chapter by chapter overview of the series. Includes vocabulary lists, questions, and links to informational Web sites.

Magic Tree House, KidsReads.com
www.kidsreads.com/series/series-magic-tree.asp
List of books and an author bio.

Magic Tree House, Random House
www.randomhouse.com/kids/magictreehouse/series.html
Publisher's Web site with an author bio, activities, and teacher and librarian resource links.

History

History for Kids
www.bbc.co.uk/history/forkids/
An appealing British history site appropriate for students.

The Mummy Maker
www.bbc.co.uk/history/ancient/egyptians/mummy_maker_game.shtml
An interactive game that tests students' knowledge of mummy-making.

(See page 58 for more history Web sites.)

Ground Level Tree Houses

Portable Playhouse, FamilyFun
familyfun.go.com/decorating-ideas/building/feature/famf0902_proj_portplay/
Directions for making a portable playhouse out of foamcore.

Fairy Tree Houses

Birds and Birdhouses
birding.about.com/od/buildhouses/
Links to a wide variety of sites giving plans for birdhouses, nest boxes, shelves, platforms, and butterfly houses.

Free Plans to Build Bird Houses

Bird Nest Gallery
www.50birds.com/GNest1.htm
Pictures of nests, links to birdhouse and nest house plans.

Bird Nests
www.backyardnature.net/birdnest.htm
A brief description of nest types with tips on how to google for nest identification.

Do It Yourself Edible Birdhouses
www.diynet.com/diy/ca_crafts_projects/article/0,2041,DIY_13721_2270233,00.html
Instructions for making birdhouses birds will eat rather than live in.

Fairy Houses of Monhegan Island
spokaneoutdoors.com/fairy.htm
Photos of Monhegan Island fairy houses.

Free Bird House Plans
www.craftybirds.com/birdhouses.html
Links to a variety of birdhouse-making sites.

Gourd Birdhouses
www.americangourdsociety.org/FAQ/birdhouse.html
Instructions for making gourd birdhouses.

Helping Mother Nature—Making Bird Houses Out of Recycled Items
www.jantjeblokhuismulder.com/articles/birdhouse.shtml
Ideas for using shoes, hats, and other items for birdhouses.

Homes for Birds
www.bcpl.net/~tross/by/house.html
Information about building nesting boxes for birds.

Books in the Magic Tree House Series

#1 Dinosaurs Before Dark

#2 The Knight at Dawn

Magic Tree House Research Guides

Co-authored by Mary Pope Osborne and Will Osborne:

Magic Tree House Research Guide: Dinosaurs

Magic Tree House: Knights and Castles

Magic Tree House Research Guide: Mummies and Pyramids

Magic Tree House Research Guide: Pirates

Magic Tree House Research Guide: Rain Forests

Magic Tree House Research Guide: Space

Magic Tree House Research Guide: Titanic

Magic Tree House Research Guide: Twisters and Other Terrible Storms

Co-authored by Mary Pope Osborne and Natalie Pope Boyce:

Magic Tree House Research Guide: Dolphins and Sharks

Magic Tree House Research Guide: Olympics of Ancient Greece

Magic Tree House Research Guide: American Revolution

Magic Tree House Research Guide: Sabertooths and the Ice Age

Magic Tree House Research Guide: Pilgrims

Junie B. Jones

Author: Barbara Park • **Illustrator:** Denise Brunkus • **Publisher:** Random House
Age Level: 6–8 years old

Irrepressible, rambunctious Junie B. Jones starts her namesake series on the first day of kindergarten. She meets her teacher (Mrs.), her two best friends (extravagantly dressed Lucille and fast-on-her-feet Grace), and her nemesis (mean Jim). At home, Junie is surrounded by a caring, though sometimes frazzled, crew of parents and grandparents. In the Junie B., First Grader series, Junie is a year older and only slightly wiser. She has a new combination of best friends and a new classroom nemesis, but she still has difficulty being the grown-up young lady she would like to think she is. The humor in the series springs from a combination of Junie B.'s stubborn and impulsive nature and her misunderstandings about the world around her. One of the nicest aspects of the Junie B. Jones series is the amused patience with which parents, teachers, and other adults respect Junie B.'s cockeyed view of the world while setting the limits necessary to guide her toward increasing self-control.

The Junie B. Jones books appeal, as read-alouds, to children as young as four, but they are most popular as early chapter books with second and third grade students. Children just a few years removed from their own kindergarten years enjoy reading about situations they have matured beyond. They very often view younger children with the same amused patience exhibited by the adults in the Junie B. books. For that reason, we think Junie B. Jones Student Buddy Days program would be the perfect complement to the series.

Junie B. Jones Student Buddy Days

The Junie B. Jones series is a perfect vehicle for enlisting older students in a program to ease the going-to-a-new-school fears of younger students. Student Buddy Days could be a one-time event, a series of events through the school year, or a weekly program that brings older students together with kindergarten students.

Student Buddy Welcome-to-the-School Party

If your school holds an orientation visit in the spring for the following year's kindergarten students, plan Student Buddy Welcome-to-the-School Day. After reading some or all of the Junie B. Jones books, enlist both the students and the kindergarten teacher in planning a party to welcome next year's kindergarten students. Decide whether the party will be in the kindergarten classroom, in the students' classroom, or in another room such as the cafeteria or library/media center. What role will the students play in the party? Ask the kindergarten teacher to talk about what might happen if the younger children are shy, fearful, or even misbehaving. It might be helpful to have the students role-play possible scenarios.

Preparation

- Ask students to discuss the kinds of fears Junie B. Jones had about school, especially in *Junie B. Jones and the Stupid Smelly Bus*. What kinds of misunderstandings and fears did your students have when they first started school? What would have been helpful for them to know?

- Have students create invitations, either individual ones for each child or the same invitation for every child (copies of an invitation created by a designated student or committee, or a winning design). Ask the office to mail the invitations with orientation information.

- Students can design a tour of the school. What parts of the school will be most important to the kindergarten students? The kindergarten classroom? The cafeteria? The library? The office? The lost and found box? The bus waiting area? How will they describe those places? (For instance, which of the following descriptions of the principal's office would create less anxiety? "The principal's office is where you go when you've been bad" or "The principal's office is where you go if you need help.")

- Have students write a list of things to know, such as the school's phone number and the amount of money kindergarten students need to bring each week for milk. The list could include a few fun things about the school, like "We have a storybook character parade in October and a holiday concert in December" or "Birds like to gather in the lilac bush outside the kindergarten classroom's window."

- Students can make name tags for themselves, the students, and the parents. (Name tags can also be filled out by one of the greeter students on the day of the party.)

Party Day

Have older students greet the incoming kindergarten students at the school's front door or in the classroom. Or, students could be stationed at the office to guide students and parents to the kindergarten classroom.

Students can assist in the kindergarten classroom by showing guests around the classroom, showing them to seats and keeping them engaged until everyone arrives. Students can also set the tables, serve, and clean up after refreshments. After the kindergarten teacher has welcomed the students and parents, your students might hold a youngster's hand while touring the building (with the understanding that some students will prefer to hold their parents' hands instead). When the party is over, your students can walk the guests to the door or, if appropriate and safe, to the parking lot.

Refreshments

A true Junie B. Jones refreshment table would consist of sugar cookies and "a beverage" (milk or juice). If the party is to be a luncheon, egg salad and tuna salad sandwiches would probably be Junie B.'s choice.

School Welcome Follow-up

With coordination and cooperation among teachers, the Junie B. Jones Buddy Day could grow into a student-buddy program:

- Older students could be paired with incoming students and meet with their "buddies" on a regular basis. Students can meet for perhaps an hour per week to do craft activities or read (the Junie B. Jones books would be a good choice).

- Student-designed materials could be part of the packet that is sent to incoming kindergarten students during the summer. The materials could include a letter of welcome, a map of the school, and a copy of the "Things to Know About the School" list. If "buddies" are assigned, a school picture or printed digital photo of the older student could be included in the packet. Photos taken of the group during the spring's orientation party would also be a nice addition.

- Students who took part in the previous spring's Welcome Party could be enlisted as greeters and guides on the first day of school. They could meet kindergarten students at the office and guide them to their classrooms at the start of the school day, then wait with them in the bus line at the end of the day.

- Students can take part in Student Buddy Celebrations throughout the school year. Possibilities include:

Student Buddy Celebration Idea #1: Pet Day

In *Junie B. Jones Smells Something Fishy,* Mrs. allowed students to bring small animals in cages and pictures of larger animals to school. Enlist students to help with a kindergarten Pet Day or Stuffed Animal Pet Day. (**Note:** All animals can be represented by pictures if there are students with pet allergies in the classroom.)

Suggested Refreshments: Animal crackers and juice.

Student Buddy Celebration Idea #2: Monster Under the Bed Day

Junie B. Jones Has a Monster Under her Bed might be a good book to read during the Halloween season. Encourage older students and their younger buddies to brainstorm ways to get rid of under-bed and in-closet monsters.

Student Buddy Celebration Idea #3: Valentine's Day Party

Recruit older students to make valentines for or with their buddies. Older students might also enjoy hosting a Valentine's Day party for the kindergarten students.

Suggested Refreshments: The refreshments served in *Junie B. Jones and the Mushy Gushy Valentine* include cupcakes, punch, and candy hearts.

A Valentine Pop-Up Card: Fold a piece of construction paper in half to make a 6" x 9" card. Decorate the front of the card with crayon, marker, or glitter glue. Cut a 5" x ½" strip of the same color construction paper. On the inside of the card, tape one edge of the strip 2" to the left of the card's center fold. Tape the other end of the strip 2" to the right of the center fold. Pull the strip gently away from the fold and close the card to crease the strip.

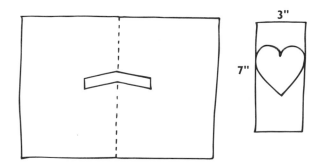

Cut a heart or flower from a 3" x 3" piece of construction paper of a different color. (The paper can be as long as 7", but not wider than 3".) Decorate the cut-out with marker, crayon, or glitter glue. Glue it to the strip, to the left of the strip's fold. Keep the card open until the glue dries.

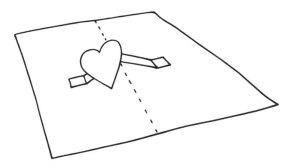

Student Buddy Celebration Idea #4: Career Day

Enlist students to help the kindergarten teacher stage a Career Day. Using the example set by Junie's class when they played Name the Tools with the janitor in *Junie B. Jones and her Big Fat Mouth,* students could create a game that includes tools used by firemen, farmers, dentists, nurses, librarians, teachers, and other community workers.

Student Buddy Celebration Idea #5: Change Your Name Day

Junie changed her name to Pinkie Gladys Gutzman in *Junie B. Jones Is a Beauty Shop Guy.* Why not declare a Change Your Name Day? Encourage students to help their buddies write their new names on name tags they have made together and toast each other's new identities with milk and cookies. This would be a good activity for April Fool's Day.

Student Buddy Celebration Idea #6: Dress Up Day

Taking inspiration from the outfit Junie wore in *Junie B. Jones Loves Handsome Warren,* encourage students to dress up in their wacky finest. Enlist older students to assist kindergarten students in making crowns and telling knock-knock jokes. (For example: Knock-Knock. Who's there? Junie. Junie Who? Junie anything else while I'm here?)

Paper Crown: Start with a 5" x 24" strip of metallic paper and triangles cut from the same metallic paper (six triangles with 3" bases and 4" sides work well). Glue or staple the triangles to the back of the strip at the top. Decorate the crown with plastic jewels, sequins, metallic star garlands, and other trimmings, or use glitter glue to create swirled designs on the crown. After the crown is dry, fit it to the wearer's head and staple or tape it to the appropriate size.

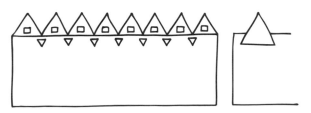

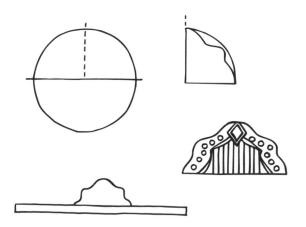

Tiara: Cut a 9" paper plate in half. Fold one of the halves in half. Cut pointed or rounded shapes on the rim side of the folded half-plate. Open the half-plate and decorate with markers, glitter glue, sequins, plastic jewels, gold braid, metallic star garlands, stickers, or other decorative elements. Glue the paper plate tiara to a 1½" x 20" strip of metallic or heavy paper. Size it to the child's head and tape or staple it accordingly.

Student Buddy Celebration Idea #7:
Combination Carnival and Field Day

Students who have read *Junie B. Jones and the Yucky Blucky Fruitcake* and *Junie B. Jones Is Captain Field Day* could come up with a list of carnival and field day games. Enlist their help in planning and running a day in which their younger buddies enjoy some of the following activities:

- Clothespin drop: Hold clothespins at waist level and drop them into a jar.

- Throwing sponges at the principal: If the weather is warm and the principal is a particularly good sport, the sponges could be wet. If not, sponges can be dry.

- Cake walk: Players walk around the room stepping on numbered squares while music plays. When the music stops, the teacher picks a number and the student who is standing on that number gets his choice of a cake or cupcake to take home.

- Chalk drawing on the sidewalk or schoolyard

- Team relay races

- Softball throw

- Skipping races

- Tug of war

Student Buddy Celebration Idea #8:
Kindergarten Graduation

Older students probably shouldn't encourage drawing polka dots on graduation gowns the way Junie and her friends did in *Junie B. Jones Is a Graduation Girl,* but they can host a graduation party to celebrate the end of their buddies' first year in school.

Suggested Refreshments: Chocolate birthday cake with white icing (because June is Junie's birth month), served with strawberry ice cream.

Simple Graduation Caps: Start with a paper or plastic bowl, suitable in size for a child's head, an 8" x 8" square of stiff paper or poster board, and two lengths of yarn, one 36" long, the other 10" long. Wrap the long piece of yarn several times around four fingers. Tie one end of the shorter length of yarn around one end of the yarn bundle. Cut the other end of the bundle to make a tassel. Poke a hole through the middle of the poster board. Pull the yarn through the hole, adjust the length of the hanging tassel, cut the yarn to size and tape the end of the yarn to the underside of the poster board. Glue the poster board to the inverted bowl. See the Web site listings for graduation cap directions.

Student Buddy Days in the Library

Student Buddy Days are easier to coordinate in a school, where groups of younger and older students are already in close proximity, but the program can also work in libraries. Create a "Junie B. Jones Reading Club" for older students, then have them plan one or all of the following events: Pet Day, Career Day, Dress Up Day, Monster-Under-the-Bed-Day, Valentine's Day Party, or Carnival and Field Day. (See the earlier list of party ideas.) Advertise the events or suggest that participants bring a sibling or friend in the 4–6 year-old age range.

The Junie B. Jones Reading Club and Buddy Program could lead very naturally to a library-sponsored babysitting course. Participants who especially enjoy working with younger students could be recruited to assist with library reading hours and craft activities.

Web Sites

The Series and Author

Junie B. Jones, KidsReads.com
www.kidsreads.com/series/series-junie.asp
Brief author bio, book list, and trivia.

Junie B. Jones, Random House
www.randomhouse.com/kids/junieb/
Publisher's Web site, includes Q and A with the author, Junie B. Jones trivia, jokes, and activities.

RIF Reading Planet, Meet the Authors and Illustrators—Barbara Park
www.rif.org/readingplanet/bookzone/content/park.mspx
Interview with Barbara Park.

Crafts

Enchanted Learning Software's Valentine Pop-Up Card
www.enchantedlearning.com/crafts/valentine/Valpopupcard.shtml
Instructions for making a Valentine pop-up.

Graduation Caps
www.thefamilycorner.com/family/kids/crafts/graduation_caps.shtml
Directions for making simple graduation caps.

Large Graduation Cap Craft
familycrafts.about.com/od/
Directions for making graduation caps.

Simple Pop-ups You Can Make!
robertsabuda.com/popmakesimple.asp
Excellent instructions for pop-up cards.

Small Graduation Cap Craft
www.dltk-holidays.com/graduation/mcap2.htm
Instructions for making graduation cap party favors.

Books in the Junie B. Jones Series

#1 *Junie B. Jones and the Stupid Smelly Bus*

#2 *Junie B. Jones and a Little Monkey Business*

#3 *Junie B. Jones and Her Big Fat Mouth*

#4 *Junie B. Jones and Some Sneaky Peeky Spying*

#5 *Junie B. Jones and the Yucky Blucky Fruitcake*

#6 *Junie B. Jones and That Meanie Jim's Birthday*

#7 *Junie B. Jones Loves Handsome Warren*

#8 *Junie B. Jones Has a Monster Under Her Bed*

#9 *Junie B. Jones Is Not a Crook*

#10 *Junie B. Jones Is a Party Animal*

#11 *Junie B. Jones Is a Beauty Shop Guy*

#12 *Junie B. Jones Smells Something Fishy*

#13 *Junie B. Jones Is (Almost) A Flower Girl*

#14 *Junie B. Jones and the Mushy Gushy Valentine*

#15 *Junie B. Jones Has a Peep in Her Pocket*

#16 *Junie B. Jones Is Captain Field Day*

#17 *Junie B. Jones is a Graduation Girl*

#18 *Junie B., First Grader (at Last!)*

#19 *Junie B., First Grader: Boss of Lunch*

#20 *Junie B., First Grader: Toothless Wonder*

#21 *Junie B., First Grader: Cheater Pants*

#22 *Junie B., First Grader: One-Man Band*

#23 *Junie B., First Grader: Shipwrecked*

#24 *Junie B., First Grader: Boo … and I Mean It!*

#25 *Junie B., First Grader: Jingle Bells, Batman Smells! (P.S. So Does May.)*

Top Secret Personal Beeswax

Captain Underpants

Author: Dav Pilkey • **Illustrator:** Dav Pilkey • **Publisher:** Scholastic
Age Level: 9–12 years old

In Dav Pilkey's Captain Underpants series, George Beard and Harold Hutchins, fourth grade students at Jerome Horwitz Elementary School, hypnotize their principal, Mr. Krupp, into thinking he is Captain Underpants. But their joke backfires in books three and four, when Mr. Krupp actually acquires super powers. Aided by Principal Krupp, who becomes Captain Underpants at the sound of fingers snapping, the two boys face the perils of attacking toilets, cafeteria ladies from outer space, Professor Poopypants, the Wicked Wedgie Woman, nasty nostril nuggets, and ridiculous robo-boogers.

The Captain Underpants series panders to one of the least endearing qualities in elementary school children—a fascination with verbal vulgarity. However, the books are also a high-energy romp through a world rich in puns, anagrams, and alternate methods of constructing narratives. The books are hybrids of written fiction and comic book graphics constructed on a solid foundation of farce.

Use the energy of the Captain Underpants books to mount a celebration that combines written, graphic, and performance arts.

Captain Underpants Bam! Wow! Socko! Multimedia Modern Art Exhibit

Create a gallery in which to display student artworks, especially those done in the styles of Dav Pilkey, Roy Lichtenstein, and other cartoon or modern artists, then plan a Gala Opening where students can show off their work to parents and friends. Encourage participants to create works depicting scenes from the Captain Underpants books, scenes from their own lives in the style of the Captain Underpants books, works depicting favorite superheroes, and pictures of teachers, parents, classmates, and themselves rendered as superheroes. Include examples of single frame or multiple frame (like a comic strip) works, sculpture, photography or multimedia (incorporating lighting, computer, and video displays), and interactive creations. Art can also be created in the form of comic books, Flip-O-Ramas, or even clothing, like superhero costumes.

Preparing for the Captain Underpants Art Exhibit

- Use shiny or fluorescent paper and cartoon typography to create words like "Splash!" "Kapow!" and "Zap!" Glue the words onto brightly colored poster board or foamcore. Add stars and outline the letters with colored markers. Hang them on the walls of the gallery, or make them double-sided and use fishing line to hang them from the ceiling.

- Create an interactive sculpture from found or recycled materials. Start with a barebones representation of Robo-George, Robot Ant 2000, the Forgetchamacallit, or one of the other characters found in the Captain Underpants books. Provide a roll of masking tape and a bin of lightweight materials (Styrofoam, coffee stirrers, bottle caps, molded plastic and paper, pipe cleaners, foam pieces, yarn, toilet paper tubes, buttons, etc.). Invite guests to add to the sculpture by attaching pieces during the gala gallery opening.

- Create an interactive Gallery Display Board whose letters can be rearranged the way George and Harold often rearrange the letters on the message board at Jerome Horwitz Elementary School. Bulletin boards with magnetized letters are available in toy stores.
- Mount a multimedia art installation by creating and filming a Captain Underpants puppet show. Set up a portable DVD player or other screening equipment in the gallery to play the puppet show continuously.

A Captain Underpants Puppet Show

Choose a favorite scene from the Captain Underpants series. Create simple stick puppets by selecting illustrations from the Captain Underpants books and copying them, either by hand, using tracing paper, or on a copy machine. If a copy machine is used, the illustrations can be enlarged. Color the figures with markers or paint, then glue them onto stiffer sheets of paper or poster board, if necessary. Cut around the figures' outlines and glue them to craft sticks. Use the sticks to make the figures move across the stage. Use the same construction method for objects, like the double-decker wedding cake that meets a bad end during Principal Krupp and Miss Ribble's narrowly averted wedding, or for ACTION! TERROR! LAUGHS! POW! BAM! elements.

Ideas for Stick Puppets

Create a puppet theater to frame the action. This can be as simple as a cardboard box with the back and part of the bottom cut away and a large opening cut in the front. Set it on a table covered with a tablecloth to hide the puppeteers, or, since this is not a live-action performance, simply frame the scene with

the camera so the puppeteers are not visible. Create backdrops by drawing the scene on a large piece of white paper, coloring it, and taping the paper to the back of the cardboard theater.

Select a narrator to explain the action, or film explanatory cartoon panels that are taped to a wall. Linger on each panel long enough to give viewers abundant time to read them when the film is shown.

In addition to puppets, use masked actors. Choose full-face illustrations from the Captain Underpants books and duplicate them using your copy machine's enlargement options. (The enlarged copies might have to be enlarged in order to render the illustrations big enough to be used as a mask.) Glue the illustrations to heavier paper or poster board, then color and cut out the masks. Carefully cut out holes for eyes. Either glue the illustrations to craft sticks so actors can hold them in front of their faces, or punch a hole near the edge of each side of the face and knot one end of a length of elastic or a rubber band at each hole. Combining actors and puppets in the same production will eliminate the need to find an actor willing to perform the title role in his underwear.

Stand-Up Superheroes

Divide participants into two-person teams to create Stand-Up Superheroes. While one of the team members (the model) lies on a large sheet of white drawing paper and assumes a superhero pose (triumphant, taking off, flying, etc.), the other team member traces around the model's body with a pencil. Glue a combination of contact paper, glossy and fluorescent papers, wallpaper, or fabric onto the figure and highlight details with boldly colored markers and paints. Glue the finished superhero onto heavy cardboard. Have an adult cut the cardboard around the figure's outline using an X-acto knife or box cutter. Hang the figure from the ceiling or make it freestanding by adding a cardboard easel.

Use the scaled diagram pictured here as a pattern for your cardboard easel. Cut the easel from an 18" x 24" piece of heavy cardboard and attach the Superhero with double-sided or heavy tape.

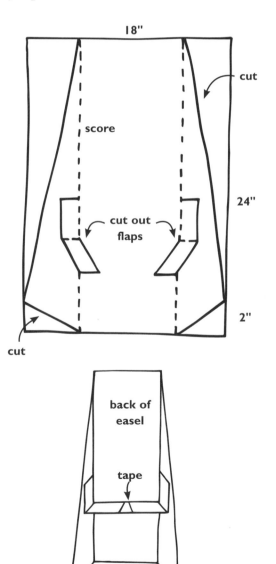

Advertising the Gala Opening

Invite participants to create posters to advertise the gallery's gala opening. Send out invitations on toilet paper, toilet paper rolls, or pieces of paper shaped like underpants.

Make gallery booklets by photographing the artwork with a digital camera, laying out the photos on a computer screen, and printing the pages.

The Gala Opening Night (or Day)

- The classiest of gallery openings have music. If you are lucky enough to have a school jazz band, recruit their participation. Perhaps some of your participants have musical parents who'd be willing to play jazz, classical, and/or superhero themes. If you cannot recruit live musicians, use CDs to supply background music.

- Write "Yow!" "Splat!" "Yikes!" and other exclamations on inflated balloons. Hang the balloons from the ceiling or, if they are filled with helium, let them float around the room anchored to cardboard cutouts of Captain Underpants. Give the balloons to guests, especially children, as they leave the gallery.

- Give everyone who enters the gallery a name tag, but use the names they would be assigned under Professor Poopypants's naming system. The three-part names, determined by the first letter of the first name and the first and last letters of the last name, can be devised by consulting the list at the end of *Captain Underpants and the Perilous Plot of Professor Poopypants: The Fourth Epic Novel,* or by visiting the Web site for Professor Poopypants' Name Change-O-Chart 2000 (see page 33).

Refreshments

There are a number of nauseating food ideas to be found in the pages of the Captain Underpants books. Some of the least objectionable include:

- Extra Strength Super Power Juice: Any juice or soda, or a punch made by combining equal amounts of juice and soda over sherbet.

- Anti-Evil Zombie Nerd Root Beer: Any cans or bottles of root beer with new Anti-Evil Zombie Nerd Root Beer labels pasted on them.

- Peanut butter and gummy worm sandwiches.

- Tuna salad with chocolate chips and miniature marshmallows.

- Potato chips served with whipped cream and chocolate sprinkles.

- Creamed chipped beef (the weapon of choice against talking toilets) served with melba toast or crackers.

Additional Captain Underpants-related Refreshments

- Captain Underpants cookies (gingerbread man cookies with white icing underpants)

- Captain Underpants open-faced sandwiches (Cut a slice of wheat bread with a gingerbread man cookie cutter, decorate it with cream cheese underpants, and lay the figure on top of a cape made of a triangle of American cheese or a slice of red pepper.)

- Toilet plunger hors d'oeuvres (Cut red grapes in half, place the halves face down, and push a thin pretzel stick into the top of each grape half.)

pretzel sticks

grape halves

Table Decorations

Decorate the refreshment table with Death-Defying Dandelions of Doom.

Death-Defying Dandelion of Doom

Fold a 9" paper plate in half. Use an X-acto knife or scissors to cut through both layers of the plate as shown in the illustration. Leave ½" of the plate's rim intact on each side of the

teeth. Open the plate. Fold both teeth rims down. Make a small hole for a dowel in the center of the plate. Cut short pieces of yellow crepe paper with pinking shears or decorative-edge scissors. Glue the crepe paper pieces to the center of the plate. Glue googly eyes to white pompoms, then glue the eyes to the plate. Add strips of black crepe paper for eyebrows.

Push a green florist's dowel (or a wooden dowel painted green) through the underside of the plate, making sure the teeth are in front of the dowel. Use masking tape to secure the plate to the dowel. Glue green construction paper leaves to the underside of the plate and to the dowel. Stand the dowel in a 4" pot packed with newspaper. Hide the newspaper with a layer of tissue or crepe paper.

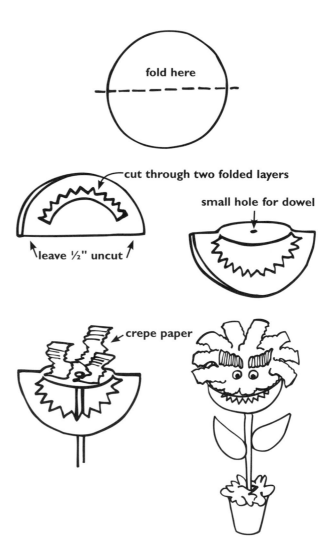

fold here

cut through two folded layers

small hole for dowel

leave ½" uncut

crepe paper

Web Sites

The Series and Author

CNN.com Book News—Captain Underpants
archives.cnn.com/2000/books/news/07/11/
captain.underpants/
An article on the Captain Underpants series.

Dav Pilkey, Kidsreads.com
www.kidsreads.com/authors/au-pilkey-dav.asp
Author bio and interview.

Dav Pilkey's Extra-Crunchy Web Site O' Fun
www.pilkey.com/index.php
The author's official Web site includes author bio, interviews, a book list, and interactive games.

The Online Adventures of Captain Underpants, Kids Fun Online
www.scholastic.com/captainunderpants
The publisher's Web site includes sophisticated graphics, interactive games, and a page for making and sending personalized Captain Underpants comic e-books.

Professor Poopypants' Name Change-O-Chart 2000
www.scholastic.com/captainunderpants/
namechanger.htm
An automatic translator of names into Poopypantese.

When Hamsters Attack! Dav Pilkey
www.whenhamstersattack.com/index.php

Puppets

Puppet Crafts
www.daniellesplace.com/html/puppets.html
Directions for sock, paper, and paper bag puppets.

The Topic: Puppets
www.42explore.com/puppet.htm
Links to Web sites that feature puppet-making ideas and scripts.

Books in the Captain Underpants Series

The Adventures of Captain Underpants: An Epic Novel

Captain Underpants and the Attack of the Talking Toilets: Another Epic Novel

Captain Underpants and the Invasion of the Incredibly Naughty Cafeteria Ladies from Outer Space (and the Subsequent Assault of the Equally Evil Lunchroom Zombie Nerds)

Captain Underpants and the Perilous Plot of Professor Poopypants: The Fourth Epic Novel

Captain Underpants and the Wrath of the Wicked Wedgie Woman: The Fifth Epic Novel

Captain Underpants and the Big Bad Battle of the Bionic Booger Boy, Part 1: The Night of the Nasty Nostril Nuggets

Captain Underpants and the Big Bad Battle of the Bionic Booger Boy, Part 2: Revenge of the Ridiculous Robo-boogers

The Captain Underpants Extra-Crunchy Book O' Fun

The All New Captain Underpants Extra Crunchy Book of Fun 2

The Adventures of Super Diaper Baby: The First Graphic Novel

The Zack Files

Author: Dan Greenburg • **Illustrator:** Jack E. Davis • **Publisher:** Penguin Putnam
Age Level: 7–10 years old

Ten-year-old Zack Greenburg, who lives with his divorced father in New York City, has numerous adventures of the mildly supernatural kind. From Bigfoot at summer camp and Elvis-impersonating turnips in the refrigerator, to insane orthodontists and alien space girls looking for mayonnaise fuel, he can barely astral-travel across town without bumping into a cat who is the reincarnation of his grandfather.

The thirty books now in the series spoof our culture's superstitions. Play along with that vein of humor by staging the Zack Files Paranormal Convention.

The Zack Files Paranormal Convention

Like paranormal experiences themselves, the Zack Files Paranormal Convention can be expanded or altered to suit the needs of your school or library. It can be:

- A relatively simple activity, with each child creating a display depicting the paranormal event in his or her favorite Zack File book and sharing it with the class.

- An event that includes some science fair elements, with participants providing factual information about events, like cloning and the possibility of time travel, in their favorite Zack Files books.

- A Halloween party that celebrates or spoofs the paranormal.

- A superstition bash that clearly debunks paranormal claims.

- A gathering (like a Star Wars convention) that includes a variety of displays, games, activities, and refreshments.

The Zack Files Paranormal Convention described in this chapter is based on the last suggestion in the list. Invite family members to join in the fun at this one-of-a-kind event.

Setting Up the Displays

Encourage participants to create exhibits based on the paranormal event in their favorite Zack Files book. They can display objects and posters, dress in costume, give out food or favors, or do a demonstration of mind reading, fortune telling, levitation, or magic. If there are electrical outlets available, decorate the displays with Christmas or patio lights.

Activities

Paranormal Beliefs Checklist

Hand out checklists of paranormal phenomena (ghosts, astral travel, UFOs, the healing power of crystals, Bigfoot, etc.) and ask participants to check the ones they believe to be true. Assign someone the task of tallying the results as the checklists are handed in. Or mount a large poster listing the phenomenon and ask people to put a check mark next to those they believe to be true.

Celebrity Fruit and Vegetable Look-alike Contest

In the spirit of *Elvis the Turnip … and Me,* invite participants to enter fruits and vegetables in a celebrity look-alike competition. Specify whether the produce is to be natural or "enhanced" (where participants decorate the produce with markers, yarn, etc.), or have a category for each. Label all the "contestants" with the names of their celebrity counterparts and hand out prizes (such as golden turnips).

Elvis the Turnip … and Me Impersonator's Circle

Rent or borrow a karaoke machine and a disc of Elvis Presley's music. Encourage participants to impersonate Elvis.

Fortune-Telling

Recruit a volunteer to staff a Fortune-telling Fishbowl of Possible Doom table. The fishbowl could contain fortunes that read, "You are doomed to become a grown-up," "You will soon be forced to make your bed," or "I see a very bad meatloaf in your future."

Zap! I'm a Mind Reader!

Mind reading requires two people—a mind reader and an assistant. The mind reader makes a point of walking out of earshot while the assistant gathers information from the audience. The information should be a letter, a number under ten, or something that requires a "yes" or "no" response. When the mind reader returns, the assistant sits in a chair. The mind reader stands behind him, places his fingertips on the assistant's temples (to better facilitate the transfer of psychic energy required for the difficult task of mind reading), and asks the question, "What number are you thinking of?" The assistant clenches his teeth together the number of times needed to indicate the number. This causes the muscles in his temple to tighten, allowing his mind to be read. The system works with "yes" and "no" questions (one for "yes," two for "no") and letters of the alphabet (count the letters from A until the correct letter is arrived at).

Stargazing

If the Zack Files Paranormal Convention is to be held at night, recruit members of a local Astronomy Club to set up outdoor telescopes and lead a stargazing demonstration.

Ghost Stories

Outside, in the dark, is also a good place to tell ghost stories. Recruit a storyteller who can spin a spooky story that stops just short of sending young children screaming into the night.

Games

Mummy Wrap Race

Divide contestants into two-person teams. Give each team a roll of toilet paper and 10 magic amulets (plastic jewels and small figurines or paper cutouts of scarabs and jewels). One team member is the mummy. Her role is to stand still with her hands crossed across her chest. The other team member is the mummy-maker. Her role is to wrap the mummy with toilet paper, making sure to incorporate all of the amulets in the wrapping. The first team to wrap its roll of toilet paper around its mummy wins. A special prize could be awarded for neatness.

Bozo the Clone

The player designated to be the Original faces the group of clones and performs a gesture (e.g., finger touches nose). The clones repeat the gesture. The Original repeats the first gesture and adds another (finger touches nose, then elbow). The clones repeat both gestures. The game continues with an additional gesture every round until none of the clones can repeat the sequence. The game can also be played to music, with the gestures being dance steps.

Bozo the Clone Rhythm Game

All of the players sit in a circle. The first player makes a rhythmic movement (hand-clapping, knee-slapping, finger-snapping, tongue-clucking). The second player repeats the movement, then adds to it. The third player repeats both movements and adds a third. If a player fails to repeat all of the elements in the correct order, he is eliminated from the game. The game continues, with every player repeating the sequence and adding to it until all but one player has been eliminated.

Scavenger Hunts

Variation 1—Food Scavenger Hunt

Make refreshments the goal of the hunt. Station one food or beverage at every Zack Files exhibit. Provide guests with a paper plate, a checklist of foods, and a pencil, and encourage them to check the foods they find as they make their way around the Zack Files Paranormal Convention. See the list of food suggestions in the Refreshments section of this chapter.

Variation 2—Gift Scavenger Hunt

Provide small gifts, like pencils, erasers, and novelty items available from party supply stores. Give out lists of items that can be found, and encourage guests to look for them as they visit the exhibits at the Zack Files Paranormal Convention. Provide a simple list, with pictures, for young children. Provide brown paper lunch bags, perhaps with a potato stamp logo of the convention on its side, in which to collect the items.

Variation 3—Word Scramble Scavenger Hunt

Tell guests to collect a slip of paper from every booth. Every slip of paper will contain one word or punctuation mark. When all of the words are collected, they can be assembled to create a sentence. (Provide a table where guests can assemble their sentences and scotch tape to secure the final sequence.) The sentence could read, "Congratulations! You have successfully collected all the pieces you need to win a prize." The assembled sentence could then be turned in for a prize. Alternatively, the sentence could read, "You have earned the right to compete for tonight's door prize. Write your name on this paper and put it in the box."

All of the Above: Give Food Scavenger Hunt lists to adults and Gift Scavenger Hunt lists to young children. Specify that the Word Scramble Scavenger Hunt is open to children under the age of 14.

Refreshments

Use these ideas for Zack-related refreshments, or encourage participants and volunteers to invent their own.

Great Grandpa's in the Litter Box

- Kitty Litter Cake: A recipe for Kitty Litter Cake is available online at KidsKuisine.com. See page 39 for the full address.

Through the Medicine Cabinet

- Cupcakes or small squares of cake with a short word written in backward lettering— "Hi" rendered as "iH."

- Big Banana Chips or Big Banana Muffins (Zack finds himself living in the "Big Banana" instead of the "Big Apple").

A Ghost Named Wanda

- Peanut M&Ms. (The ghost used them to spell out answers to Zack's questions.)

- Ghost Dip: Make a ghost out of a small head of cauliflower cut in half. Lay it on its cut side. Cut a green grape in half. Attach the grape eyes to the cauliflower with cream cheese or toothpicks. If desired, add a strip of green pepper for a mouth. Set the cauliflower in the middle of a bowl and surround it with a white dip, like ranch or blue cheese. Three slender strips of green pepper tied together at one end with a twist tie can be stuck into the dip to look like the ghost's hand gripping the edge of the bowl. Serve with vegetable crudités or chips.

Zap! I'm a Mind Reader

- Tarantulas: Insert thin pretzel stick legs into a donut hole body.

- Shocking Punch: Put sparkling seltzer into a clear punch bowl with an ice mold containing "wires" of thin licorice (or the ice ring could contain gummy worm electric eels).

Dr. Jekyll, Orthodontist

- Dr. Jekyll's Chocolate Mouthwash: Chocolate milk or Yoo-Hoo chocolate drink.

I'm Out of My Body … Please Leave a Message

- Lemon Fizz: A combination of lemonade and tonic or soda water.

Never Trust a Cat who Wears Earrings

- Open-face Mummy Sandwiches: Cut a piece of white or wheat bread in half to make two rectangular mummy cases. Cut the corners to shape them a bit. Spread with butter or soft cream cheese. On each mummy case, place a square of cheese, trimmed at the corners (that will be the gold mask). Decorate the mask and mummy body with cheese in a tube and bits of olive, pimento, pickle, and red and green peppers.

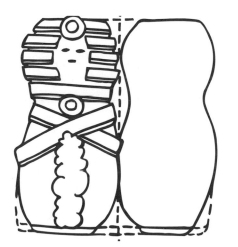

My Son, the Time Traveler

- Dates or Date Nut Bread

- Mack's Snacks: Cocktail franks. (Zack is shocked that his son from the future has never tasted a hot dog.)

The Volcano Goddess Will See You Now

- Pineapple upside-down cake or muffins.

- Pineapple chunks and cherries on toothpicks.

- Pineapple juice punch: Equal amounts of pineapple juice and ginger ale. Pineapple pieces or orange sherbet can be added.

Bozo the Clone

- Grape Clones: A bowl of green grapes with one grape labeled, carefully, in ink, "original."

How to Speak Dolphin in Three Easy Lessons

- Goldfish or other fish-shaped crackers or cookies.

- Reeses Peanut Butter Cups and Peanut M&Ms: (The dolphins use them to compare dolphin brain sizes to fish brain sizes.)

Now You See Me, Now You Don't

- Invisible Ink Punch: Club soda or Seltzer with lemons, limes, and cherries.

The Misfortune Cookie

- Fortune cookies.

Elvis the Turnip … and Me

- Elvis is in the Dip: A turnip carved to look like a bust of Elvis. Use food coloring and a paintbrush to color its eyes and hair. Place it in the middle of a bowl and surround it with a colorful dip that contains a lot of chopped vegetable bits. Serve with chips or vegetable crudités.

Hang a Left at Venus

- Spaceship Cookies: Cookies with a ring of chocolate chips or raisins around the edges.

Evil Queen Tut and the Great Ant Pyramids

- Pyramid with Ants: Rice Krispies® squares stacked in a pyramid. Use raisins to create a column of ants.

Yike's! Grandma's a Teenager

- Rock candy: See page 76 for directions.
- Candy bracelets.

How I Fixed the Year 1000 Problem

- Chunks of crusty bread with humus dip.

The Boy Who Cried Bigfoot

- Bigfoot Fodder: Slices of fruit and vegetables.

How I Went from Bad to Verse

- Meringues (Zack floated when he heard light verse.)
- Riki-riki cocktail: Although it was made from cricket juice in the book, we suggest fruit punch with gummy bugs.

Don't Count on Dracula

- Garlic dip with garlic bread or garlic-flavored crackers.

This Body's Not Big Enough for Both of Us

- Tea sandwiches.
- Slices of pound cake spread with lemon curd.
- Tea punch: See page 76 for directions.

Green Eggs and Dinosaurs

- Green jelly beans
- Dinosaur meat: Chunks of ham on toothpicks.

My Grandma, Major League Slugger

- Miniature Baby Ruth candy bars.

Trapped in the Museum of Unnatural History

- Vending machine foods.
- Paleolithic foods, like nuts, berries, dried fruits, and gummy worms and bugs.

Me and My Mummy

- Mummy Fingers: Soft tortillas wrapped around mozzarella sticks or cold cuts. Use a dab of cream cheese glue to apply an almond fingernail. Use spinach and roasted tomato tortillas to vary the color.

My Teacher Ate My Homework

- Tortilla homework: Use food coloring and a paintbrush to write the words "Homework" or "Book Report" on pieces of soft tortilla. Serve with garlic dip.
- Full Moon Cookies: Sugar cookies.

Tell a Lie and Your Butt will Grow

- Truth Serum: A pitcher of water or other clear liquid, or any bottled or canned soda labeled WARNING! TRUTH SERUM.

Just Add Water and Scream

- Bottled water or pitchers of ice water with lemon or lime slices.
- Spore Mix: Trail mix made with small cereals, nuts, and raisins.

It's Itchcraft

- Witch's Dip with Cat's Tongues. Black bean dip with red pepper slices for dipping.

Web Sites

The Series and Author

The Zack Files Home Page
us.penguingroup.com/static/packages/us/yreaders/zack/index.htm
Publisher's Web site. The site opens on a book order list and requires clicking on "Back to Zack Files Index" to access other features.

The Zack Files Television Program

The Zack Files
www.abc.net.au/rollercoaster/zackfiles/default.htm
The Australian Broadcasting Corporation's Web site for the Zack TV show.

The Zack Files Interactive
www.thezackfiles.com/main.html
Web site for the Zack Files TV show.

Superstitions

Cat Superstitions
www.literary-cat.cwc.net/superstition.htm
Cat superstitions.

Folklore, Superstitions, and Proverbs
www.xmission.com/~emailbox/folklore.htm
Cat superstitions in folklore.

Mummy Tombs
www.mummytombs.com
A collection of Web pages devoted to mummy information.

Scary Superstitions
www.corsinet.com/trivia/scary.html
Alphabetical listing with brief definitions of superstitions.

Superstition Bash
www.csicop.org/superstition/index.html
Ideas for holding an event spoofing superstitions.

Urban Legends Reference Pages
www.snopes.com/
Excellent site for debunking rumors of the paranormal, but it is written for adults.

Recipes

Kellogg's Recipes
www.kelloggs.ca/recipes/index.htm
Follow links to Rice Krispies Recipe Web site, the Classics, for recipes that include microwave and large quantity versions of Rice Krispies squares.

Kitty Litter cake
www.kidskuisine.com/asp/recipe.asp?recipe=104
Recipe for a Kitty Litter cake.

Books in the Zack Files Series

Hank the Cowdog

Author: John R. Erickson • **Illustrator:** Gerald L. Holmes • **Publisher:** Penguin Puffin
Age Level: 9–12 years old

Hank the Cowdog is a western cowboy canine with a grander sense of his own importance than is warranted by his abilities. That no one appreciates him for the hardworking, brilliantly deductive, irresistible-to-the-ladies animal he knows himself to be does not deter him from his self-appointed rounds as chief of security on High and Sally May Loper's Twitchell, Texas, ranch. The anthropomorphic animals that join Hank in the more than 40 books in the series include a father and son buzzard team with a disconcerting habit of vomiting when upset, a couple of dim-witted coyotes who are always on the lookout for a Hank dinner, a Mae West-like vamp of a beagle, and a chicken-hearted second-in-command of ranch security. Hank's mangling of the English language with phrases like, "Now that we've cleared the first turtle" and "It was a night not fit for man nor beets" make the books a lot of fun to read. We hope a Twitchell Barbecue will make the books a lot of fun to celebrate as well.

Twitchell Barbecue

Hold a Bar-B-Q with lots of food, music, outdoor games, and craft activities for children. Encourage participants to wear bandannas, jeans, cowboy hats, boots, and other western clothing or, better yet, come dressed as their favorite Hank the Cowdog characters. The event could be just for fun, or it could be used as a fund-raiser by selling tickets to the event or charging for food.

Food

Name that Dog

What better way to celebrate a book about dogs than to serve hot dogs? (Hank would call them weenies.) Provide condiments and instructions for name-that-dog variations: Drover (plain and lazy, no condiments); Hank (Texas spicy, with chili); Slim (baked beans); Wallace the Buzzard (all the condiments mixed together, looks like ... well, you know). Invite students and parents to invent their own combinations appropriate to the characters in the Hank the Cowdog series. Consider giving awards for the most creative hot dog inventions.

Bones

Use dog bone-shaped cookie cutters to make cookies and biscuits, or to cut toast into bone shapes.

Other Foods

Serve your favorite versions of chili, baked beans, trail mix, beef jerky, corn bread, or fritters.

Beverages

Serve sarsaparilla or root beer.

Chili/Baked Bean Contest

Hold a contest to determine the best chili and/or baked beans. Enlist parents, students, or local restaurants (or ask all three groups to participate and have a separate award for each category). Determine a minimum amount of chili or beans for each entrant to provide.

Arrange hot plates or kitchen facilities for heating and people to serve. Provide small disposable bowls and spoons for sampling, along with trash barrels for those containers. If the winners are to be chosen by popular vote, create a ballot that can be turned in for counting. If the winners are to be determined by a panel of judges, recruit the judges and set the criteria for judging. Decide if there is to be a prize beyond the honor of winning the title of Chilimaster or Beanmaster of the Twitchell Barbecue.

Music

From coyote-howling to Hank the Cowdog's laments, music is a significant part of the Hank the Cowdog series. Make it a part of the Twitchell Barbecue as well.

Western Music Sing-Along

Organize a sing-along of tunes like "Happy Trails to You," "Home on the Range," "Yellow Rose of Texas," "Deep in the Heart of Texas," "All My Exes Live in Texas," "Streets Of Laredo," "Mama, Don't Let Your Babies Grow Up to be Cowboys," "Red River Valley," "Don't Fence Me In," and other western songs. Lyrics for many western songs can be found on the Web site The Yellow Rose (and Other Songs) of Texas, listed on page 47.

Enlist students or adults to accompany the sing-along on guitars, fiddles, keyboards, and other instruments.

Encourage participants to bring homemade instruments, or give them a chance to make instruments at a crafts table. The Crafts section of this chapter has instructions for simple rain-sticks, rattles, drums, and kazoos.

Body Music

Though it does not require the construction of instruments, Body Music would benefit from a short course of instruction and some clear leadership during the sing-along. Recruit someone to be Body Music Conductor and have him or her run through the basics with the audience:

- finger-snapping
- hand-clapping
- foot-tapping and foot-stomping (The difference lies in volume and vehemence.)
- thigh-slapping
- teeth-chomping
- lip-razzing
- velcro-ripping (Everyone with Velcro on his shoes or clothing pulls the Velcro fastenings open on cue.)

Animal Music

Perhaps the Body Music Conductor can double as the Animal Music Conductor. For the second or third chorus of some of the songs, designate parts of the audience to deliver dog, coyote, cat, and buzzard versions of the music.

Square, Line, or Contra Dancing

Enlist a local square or contra dance group to give an exhibition of square, line, or contra dancing. Hold a dance, with members of the club teaching simple dances to the participants.

Cowboy Poetry

While not exactly music, poetry comes close. Enlist people to read western poetry. Invite students and adults to read their own works as part of a Western Open-Mike Poetry Slam.

Other Activities

Hank the Cowdog Balloons

Recruit an adult or older child to make balloon dogs. Directions can be found on the Magical Balloon-dude Dale Web site listed on page 47.

Food Dogs

As a tribute to Slim Chance, the cowhand who often eats Vienna sausages straight from the can, invite participants to add their contributions to a food dog sculpture exhibit. Use Vienna sausages, toothpicks, cooked and uncooked spaghetti noodles, dried peas, beans and lentils, chopped olives, pickles, vegetables, scallions (good for dog collars), and cream cheese (for glue). Make sure participants understand the figures are for display, not eating. Provide an area for hand washing when the activity is finished.

Crafts

Set aside an area for creating musical instruments to be used in the sing-along, as well as other Hank the Cowdog activities.

Drums

Simple drums can be made from:

- coffee cans or oatmeal boxes with their plastic lids taped on

- bowls with canvas, rubber, or plastic stretched tightly across the opening, then tied in place or fixed in place with a rubber band

- empty plastic milk containers turned upside down (The eraser end of pencils, or a dowel wrapped with cloth, rubber bands, or inner tubing can serve as drumsticks.)

Encourage participants to personalize their drums by gluing on construction paper and decorating with feathers, plastic jewels, and glitter.

Fingertip Drums

Fill plastic soda bottle caps with Play-Doh® or a play-clay of similar consistency. When participants push their fingers into the clay, the caps will stay on their fingers while they tap against a tabletop, floor, trash can lid, or pot to make music.

Toilet Paper Tube Kazoos

Using masking tape, fasten a 3" circle of waxed paper across one end of a cardboard toilet paper tube or a shortened paper towel tube.

Make a ½" slit in the middle of the waxed paper circle with the tip of a pair of scissors. Wrap colored paper around the tube and glue into place. (A sheet of 8½" x 11" colored paper works well. Cut into fourths, it makes four rectangles that perfectly fit most toilet paper tubes.) Decorate the kazoos with stickers, sequins, or bits of tissue paper. Participants play the kazoo by humming into the open end of the tube. (This activity can be made simpler by slitting the 3" waxed paper circles beforehand and providing pre-cut paper sized to fit the tubes.)

Paper Towel Tube Rain Sticks

Place a 3" circle of construction or other heavy paper across one end of a paper towel tube and use masking tape to fix it firmly in place. Insert several bent pipe cleaners, 10" x ½" pieces of bent, lightweight cardboard or bent drinking straws into the open end of the tube. Pour ¼ cup of dried beans, uncooked rice, or popcorn kernels into the tube. Place another 3" paper circle over the open end of the tube and fix it firmly in place with masking tape. Cover and decorate the rain stick in the same way the kazoo was decorated. Hold the completed rain stick upright, at a slight angle. When the dried beans slowly pour through the bent materials inside the paper towel roll, the rain stick will produce a sound.

bent straw, pipe cleaner, or cardboard

Rattles

Use one of these methods to create simple rattles:

- Put pebbles, dried beans, uncooked rice, or dry cereal into a paper or plastic bowl or an aluminum pie tin. Place an identical bowl or pie tin on top, open side facing down, and staple or tape the rims of the bowls together. Paper cups can also be used.

- Put pebbles, dried beans, uncooked rice, or dry cereal into plastic milk or soda containers and glue their caps into place. If the caps have been lost, cover the openings with a heavy paper circle and tape it firmly in place.

Participants can decorate their rattles by gluing on paper, glitter, yarn, and plastic jewels.

Hank the Cowdog Puppets

Each puppet requires two pudding or gelatin boxes. Remove the top flap from each box. Paint the pudding boxes pink on one large side of each box and brown on all other sides. (The pink sides are the insides of Hank's mouth.) Glue a red or pink felt tongue onto one of the pink sides, its base at the open end of the box. Put one pudding box on top of the other, pink sides together.

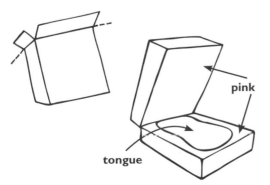

Use masking tape to tape them together along the open sides' edges to form a hinge.

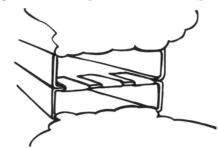

Use white glue to attach googly eyes to the box. More complicated eyes can be made by gluing the googly eyes to ½" black felt circles. Then glue the circles to 1" white pom-poms. (Eyes may be made in advance.) Glue the white pom-poms to the upper box to make Hank's eyes. Add a 1" diameter black felt circle for a nose and black or brown felt ears. Glue strips of brown crepe or tissue paper to the inside of the cut edges of the boxes to create the suggestion of Hank's body. Put your hand inside the boxes to make Hank move.

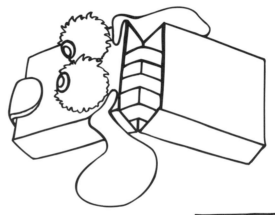

Slim Chance's Cowboy Hat

Cut an oval from a 12" x 18" sheet of construction paper. In its center, trace a 7" diameter circle. Pierce the center of the circle with the tip of a pair of scissors and cut across the circle's diameter. Repeat two more times to make six pie-shaped flaps. Fold the flaps up and place a loop of masking tape on the outside of each flap.

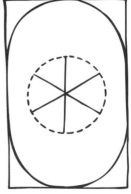

Fold a 12" x 12" sheet of construction paper in half vertically, then in half horizontally. Open the paper up and fold the corners into the center of the paper, forming a diamond shape. Pinch the pointed edges of each folded corner together and tape them to retain that pinched position. This is the crown of the hat.

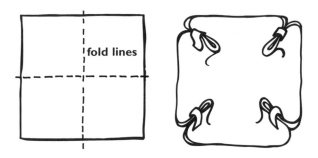

Turn the crown over and place it on top of the circle in the middle of the brim, pushing the six flaps against the inside of the crown, and gently shaping it to fit the brim. Turn the hat over. Use masking tape to secure the inside of the crown, taping over any protruding seams. Turn the hat over again. Wrap a band of construction paper, 1½" x 24", around the base of the crown, and tape it in place.

Games

Play a variety of dog-inspired, Western-style games to add some fun to your barbecue.

Winners could receive dog bone-shaped cookies made with dog bone cookie cutters as prizes.

Mystery Bandanna Game

Put an object (spoon, key, eraser, pen, etc.) into a bandanna and tie it shut. Ask participants to guess the contents. Give prizes for correct answers.

Obedience School

Adapt the rules of Simon Says to Hank the Cowdog's world. Players stand in a line facing the person who is designated to be Sally May. Sally May gives commands appropriate for dogs such as lie down, beg for a treat, roll over, bark, scratch your ear, wag your tail, growl, pant, etc. Players must only obey commands that start with the words "Sally May Says." If someone obeys a command that does not start with those words, he or she is out of the game. The game continues until there is only one good dog left. That player is the winner.

Cattle-Branding

Adapt Pin the Tail on the Donkey to a western theme by pinning a brand on a cow. Start by making the target. (Draw the outline of a cow on a sheet of brown craft paper or a brown paper grocery bag, draw a red X on the cow's flank, then cut the cow out and tape it to a wall at waist-level for the age group expected to play the game.)

Next, make Brands. Use a compass to draw circles on a sheet of paper. Twelve circles with 3" diameters will fit on an 8½" x 11" sheet of paper. Draw large block letters inside the circles. Invite participants to choose a circle with a letter, cut it out, and color it. Some circles can be left blank for participants who want to make their own unique brand.

To play, blindfold a student and give him or her a potato masher onto which a brand has been affixed. (Use a small loop of cellophane tape on the front of the brand to make it stick to the masher. Use a larger loop of masking tape on the back of the brand. When the child pushes the potato masher against the wall, the masking tape will adhere to the cow, separating the brand from the masher.) The child holds the masher by the handle and tries to brand the cow. When the game is over, the winner is the cowboy whose brand is closest to the X on the cow's flank.

Cattle Roundup

Two players are cowdogs. The rest are cows. The cowdogs hold opposite ends of a length of rope or a hula hoop, with which they attempt to surround cows and lead them to an area designated as the corral. Cows try to elude capture. (They cannot duck under the rope or hoop once they have been caught.) The game ends when all of the cows are in the corral.

Cattle Drive

Play this game outdoors with plenty of room and many participants. Divide the players into cows and cowboys. There should be three or four times more cows than cowboys. (Since it takes two children to make every cow, that means six to eight children will be cows for every child who is a cowboy.)

Cows consist of two children, one with his hands on his head and two fingers extended to form horns. The other child holds onto the first child's hips. Cows walk unless there is a stampede.

Cowboys twirl an imaginary lariat in one hand, hold imaginary reins in the other hand, and skip to imitate the motion of being on horseback.

The cowboys work together to drive the cattle from the ranch at one end of the field to the Twitchell Livestock Auction at the other end of the field. The cows wish only to wander around the field eating grass.

When a cowboy rides alongside a cow, touches it, and says, "Gitalong, little dogie" that cow must move with the cowboy and become part of the herd.

To make the game more lively, a Game Leader calls out orders. Orders include:

- **Stampede!** The first cow in the group leads a mad dash of cattle from the herd. Cowboys can regain control of the herd by tagging each cow and saying "Whoa, dogie!" (a command to stop) and "Gitalong, little dogie" (a command to follow).

- **Mavericks!** Cows reverse themselves, head players becoming tail players, and move in the opposite direction.

- **River Crossing.** Cowboys must keep cows in a single line while crossing a river. The river can be made by laying two parallel lengths of rope on the ground, 5 to 15 feet apart.

- **Canyon.** Cowboys must keep cattle together while passing through an opening made by placing chairs on the field.

- **Bed 'em Down!** Cowboys circle the herd and sing to them.

Variations of Cattle Drive

Variation 1: Choose a few students to be rustlers. Rustlers can steal cows by tagging them and saying, "Gitalong, little dogie." Cowboys must chase the rustlers off and recover their livestock by tagging the cows and saying "Gitalong, little dogie." A rustler who is tagged by a cowboy is sent to jail and is, therefore, out of the game.

Variation 2: Play the game with more than one herd of cattle and crew of cowboys. Cows can get accidentally mixed into the other herds, or cowboys can steal each other's cows. The team that arrives at the livestock auction with the most cows wins the game.

"Cattle Drive" is an embellished version of a game from the Insane Scouter Web site (see page 47).

Steal the Steak

Half of the players in this game are dogs and half are cowboys or cowgirls. The steak can be a deflated football, an old brown shoe, or a piece of cardboard painted to look like a steak. At the start of the game, the steak is on a rock or chair that is designated to be the Grill. Other parts of the game field are designated Doghouse and Dog Pound.

Goal of the game: A dog that reaches the Doghouse with the steak without being tagged by a cowboy wins the game. The cowboys win if all the dogs are in the Dog Pound and the steak is still on the Grill.

How to play: The steak is placed on the Grill. The dogs attempt to steal the steak and take it to the Doghouse. When a dog takes the steak he can be tagged by one of the cowboys. A dog who is tagged while carrying the steak goes to the Dog Pound and is out of the game. The steak remains where the dog dropped it until it is picked up and returned to the Grill by a cowboy or is snatched by another dog. Dogs may toss the steak to one other. Only dogs that have the steak in their possession when tagged are out of the game.

Contests

Best Costumes

Encourage participants to come to the barbecue in costume. Award individual prizes for the best Hank, Alfred, Wallace, Pete, Slim Chance, High Loper, and Sally May costumes. Award group prizes for the best Hank and Friends combinations. Photograph the costumed participants for later display.

Animal Communication Contests

Invite participants to compete for Top Cowdog status in a barking contest, with prizes awarded for Loudest, Most Melodious, and Most Realistic. Similarly, invite participants to compete for Conquering Coyote, Best Buzzard, Finest Feline, and Most Marvelous Moos honors. Dog, cat, coyote, cow, and buzzard sounds can be heard online at several of the sites listed on pages 46–47.

Co-op Dog Food Eating Contest

The winner is the participant who can eat all of the co-op dog food (a dry, relatively tasteless cereal) in his bowl in the shortest amount of time. Fill the bowls with equal amounts of dry cereal. (New dog food bowls would be a nice touch, but plastic soup bowls would work well, too.) Instruct contestants to hold their hands behind their backs and start eating when the game leader calls, "Start." When a contestant finishes every morsel of his or her cereal, he or she holds his or her hands in the air and the game leader calls, "Stop." All contestants stop eating.

As a variation, invite participants to drink water out of clean bowls while they hold their hands behind their backs. The contestant who drinks all of the water in his or her bowl first is the winner.

Web Sites

The Series and Author

Hank the Cowdog
www.hankthecowdog.com/

Western Costumes and Crafts

Bull-Riding Cowboy
familyfun.go.com/arts-and-crafts/season/feature/famf108costume/famf108costume2.html

Convincing Cowboy and Wild West Cowgirl
www.sesameworkshop.org/aboutus/newsletter_article.php?contentId=111000

Craft Topic: Cowboy Hats
www.thebestkidsbooksite.com/craftdetails.cfm?TopicID=245

Activities and Games

Insane Scouter, Boy Scouts of America
www.insanescouter.com

Magical Balloon-dude Dale
www.mbd2.com/kidsstuff.htm

Texas

Lone Star Junction
www.lsjunction.com/

The Yellow Rose (and Other Songs) of Texas
www.lsjunction.com/midi/songs.htm

Animals

Cow Sounds
cowabash51.topcities.com/COWSOUNDS/
cowsounds.html

Dogs at Enchanted Learning
www.enchantedlearning.com/themes/dog.
shtml

JungleWalk.com
www.junglewalk.com/frames.asp

Turkey Vulture Photograph and Sound Recordings
mirror-pole.com/collpage/tv/tv.htm

Books in the Hank the Cowdog Series

#1 The Original Adventures of Hank the Cowdog

#2 The Further Adventures of Hank the Cowdog

#3 It's a Dog's Life

#4 Murder in the Middle Pasture

#5 Faded Love

#6 Let Sleeping Dogs Lie

#7 The Curse of the Incredible Priceless Corncob

#8 The Case of the One-Eyed Killer Stud Horse

#9 The Case of the Halloween Ghost

#10 Every Dog Has His Day

#11 Lost in the Dark Unchanted Forest

#12 The Case of the Fiddle-Playing Fox

#13 The Wounded Buzzard on Christmas Eve

#14 Hank the Cowdog and Monkey Business

#15 The Case of the Missing Cat

#16 Lost in the Blinded Blizzard

#17 The Case of the Car-Barkaholic Dog

#18 The Case of the Hooking Bull

#19 The Case of the Midnight Rustler

#20 The Phantom in the Mirror

#21 The Case of the Vampire Cat

#22 The Case of the Double Bumblebee Sting

#23 Moonlight Madness

#24 The Case of the Black-Hooded Hangman

#25 The Case of the Swirling Killer Tornado

#26 The Case of the Kidnapped Collie

#27 The Case of the Night-Stalking Bone Monster

#28 The Case of the Mopwater Files

#29 The Case of the Vampire Vacuum Sweeper

#30 The Case of the Haystack Kitties

#31 The Case of the Vanishing Fishhook

#32 The Garbage Monster from Outer Space

#33 The Case of the Measled Cowboy

#34 Slim's Good-Bye

#35 The Case of the Saddle House Robbery

#36 The Case of the Raging Rottweiler

#37 The Case of the Deadly Ha-Ha Game

#38 The Fling

#39 The Secret Laundry Monster Files

#40 The Case of the Missing Bird Dog

#41 The Case of the Shipwrecked Tree

#42 The Case of the Burrowing Robot

#43 The Case of the Twisted Kitty

#44 The Dungeon of Doom

#45 The Case of the Falling Sky

#46 The Case of the Tricky Trap

#47 The Case of the Tender Cheeping Chickies

A Series of Unfortunate Events

Author: Lemony Snicket (Daniel Handler) • **Illustrator:** Brett Helquist
Publisher: HarperCollins • **Age Level:** 9–12 years old

A Series of Unfortunate Events combines the out-of-the-frying-pan-into-the-fire excitement of a Perils-of-Pauline adventure with a darkly Victorian sensibility reminiscent of Edward Gorey. Orphaned siblings Violet, Klaus, and Sunny Baudelaire must depend on each other to escape the murderous clutches of their cousin Count Olaf because the adults who should be protecting them are singularly inept. Throughout the series, Violet, a 14-year-old with a genius for inventing, Klaus, a 12-year-old with a voracious appetite for reading, and Sunny, a baby with extremely sharp teeth, use their talents to escape the tragedies that often include the demise of their guardians. The series starts with three orphans searching for a safe home, then becomes increasingly focused on their search for the truth about their parents' deaths.

An extra book, *Lemony Snicket: The Unauthorized Autobiography*, appeared midway through the publication of the series' projected thirteen volumes. At first read, it is a cobbled-together explanation of Lemony Snicket's identity that does little to illuminate the author, but, beneath the romp of obfuscation lies one clear call to readers: observe the world around you.

Searching and observing, the two actions that lie at the heart of A Series of Unfortunate Events, make the books a perfect companion to the increasingly popular pastime of letterboxing.

Letterboxing with Lemony Snicket

Letterboxing dates back more than a hundred years in Great Britain, but it has become a popular activity in the United States only in the past few years. In its simplest form, a letterbox consists of a "stash"—a notebook, a stamp pad, and a distinctive stamp inside a waterproof container. The person who makes the letterbox places it somewhere out of open view but accessible to those who know where to look, then creates a clue for others to follow. Searchers carry their own notebooks, stamps, and stamp pads. When a searcher finds a letterbox, she opens it, uses her own stamp to leave an impression in the letterbox's notebook, uses the letterbox's stamp to leave an impression in her notebook, puts the stash back into the waterproof container, and replaces it where she found it. Letterboxing combines puzzle-solving, exploring, and collecting—all activities that reinforce observation skills.

Letterboxing draws together a nationwide group of participants who search for clues on Internet Web sites like the Letterboxing North America WebRing. However, it is also possible to create a local, private letterboxing activity. That's what we suggest for your Lemony Snicket celebration. The event can be held indoors in your school or library, or outdoors in various locations in your community, depending on your available resources and time frame.

Creating Stamps

Every letterbox will require a different stamp, and every participant in the letterboxing activity will need a distinctive stamp as well. Stamps can be purchased, or they can be made in stamp-making workshops before the letterboxing activity begins.

Craft Foam Sheet Stamps: Make simple stamps by cutting shapes from craft foam sheets or assembling pre-cut craft foam shapes into designs and gluing the pieces onto the top of a film canister or block of wood.

Moldable Foam Stamps: Stamps can be made from sheets of moldable foam stamp material, available at craft stores or online. Pieces of the foam can be engraved with a pencil point or pressed against objects, like coins or leaves, and heated with a hair dryer. The foam is then glued to blocks of wood or jar lids to create personalized stamps.

Gum Eraser Stamps: Start with a gum eraser (the tan, more crumbly erasers found in art and office supply stores), a butter knife, an unsharpened pencil, pliers, and a few toothpicks. Draw a design on one large side of the eraser and carve its outline with the butter knife. For finer detail, make a tool by pulling the eraser out of the end of the pencil with a pair of pliers. Use the metal pencil end to carve the edges of the stamp and make large round holes. For a tool that will carve more finely, crimp the metal end of the pencil with the pliers. Use toothpicks for creating smaller holes and details.

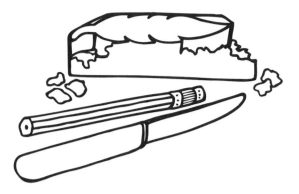

More detailed instructions for gum eraser stamps, as well as instructions for stamps that can be made from bunion and corn pads, can be found at the Letterboxing Kids section of the Letterboxing North America WebRing (see page 54).

Creating Notebooks

Every participant will need a notebook. Ask each participant to bring a notebook to the pre-letterboxing workshop, or provide notebooks for everyone, along with colored markers and glitter glue that they can use to personalize them. Devote at least one notebook page to each letterbox in the activity. Label the pages with the names of the books. Leave space on the pages to record the clues, where the boxes were found, and imprints of the boxes' stamps.

Technically, participants do not need their own stamp pads because every letterbox will contain a stamp pad. However, participants might prefer to have their own stamp pads in case the stamp pad in the letterbox is too dry to use, or in order to stamp with colors of their own choosing.

Assembling the Letterboxes

You will need a waterproof plastic container for each book in A Series of Unfortunate Events (12 have been published; eventually there will be 13 total). Rubbermaid and Tupperware-type storage boxes with tight-fitting lids are good for this purpose. They need to be large enough to contain the letterbox's notebook, stamp, and stamp pad. Plastic bags, preferably ziplock bags, give the notebooks even more protection inside the containers.

Assemble a box for each book in the series. Into each box put a notebook with the name of the book on its cover, a stamp with an imprint that relates to an event in the book, and a stamp pad. Label the cover of each box with information like this: "Sunnydale Library/ Lemony Snicket Letterboxing Hunt/Box 5/ The Austere Academy." You might want to add a note for people who accidentally discover the box: "This box is part of a literature celebration being conducted by Sunnydale Library's Children's Room. Please leave it as you found it. Thanks!" Use clear package tape to affix the labels to the box.

Placing the Letterboxes

Decide on a location for each box. Make sure the locations are safe and within an appropriate radius for the children who will be participating. Secure permission if the boxes are going to be placed on private, and even some public, property and be sensitive to the damage participants might unwittingly cause while searching. (Don't put the boxes in flower gardens.) Letterboxes don't have to be located outdoors. They can be located inside schools, libraries, and public buildings. Where theft might be a problem, boxes can be left in the guardianship of goodhearted teachers, librarians, city workers, and local merchants.

Creating Clues

The locations of the boxes and the clues to find them will depend on the surroundings you have to work with. Later in this chapter we'll give a list of clue and stamp ideas for each book in the series, but the best way to personalize your letterboxing activity is to assemble a brainstorming group of young and adult Lemony Snicket fans from your own area.

For each letterbox, create a clue that relates to its corresponding book. For instance, in the series' fifth book, *The Austere Academy,* the orphans are sent to a school whose motto is "Memento Mori" ("Remember you will die").

The clue for the location of box five could be a simple direction: "Go through the front gates of Locust Grove Cemetery, turn right at the angel monument. Box five is located near a polished black granite headstone labeled 'Smith.'"

If the participants are more sophisticated, the clues can be more complicated: "Memento mori: enter the gates with that in mind, turn right with wings to guide you, and find box five near a stone that glows like a black sapphire in the sun."

Clues can be written in Lemony Snicket's pedantic style: "Go through the front gates of Locust Grove Cemetery. ('Gates' in this instance means an opening in a wall, not a moveable structure that swings on hinges that might, in other circumstances, occupy that opening.) Turn right (which in this instance means 'not left,' rather than 'not incorrect') and find box five near a black headstone (which in this instance means a grave marker, not a stone that resembles a head)."

The clues can also be written as letters or fragments from one of the Baudelaire's notebooks or one of Isadora Quagmire's couplets: "Memento mori—You will die. / Through those gates go you and I. / Right past an angel's feathered wing / To a black glow, like a sapphire ring."

Letterboxing

The easiest way to make clues available to participants is to create a list of clues, then make copies and distribute them. If all of the participants are going to search on the same day, ask them to stagger the time they start, or begin their searches at a different box number on the list. More people can participate, and they can do it at their leisure, if the letterbox search is not a one-day event. Make the clues available on the school or library Web site, or in flyers that are available in the library or classroom. Allow a week, a month, or all summer, for participants to find the letterboxes and collect stamp imprints in their notebooks. If the activity continues for a length of time, ask participants to report missing letterboxes or dry stamp pads so those boxes or materials can be replaced.

End Letterboxing with Lemony Snicket by collecting the letterboxes and having a party, during which participants can compare notebooks and stamp each other's notebooks with their own stamps.

Locations, Clues, and Stamp Ideas

The locations, clues, and stamp designs you use will depend on what is available to you. Use the following list to devise those that match your resources.

Common Threads in A Series of Unfortunate Events

Count Olaf's Eye: A symbol that is tattooed on the count's ankle, this shows up repeatedly through the series, often giving away the villain's disguises. Locations that feature an eye, or even an "I," could be worked into the clues.

Violet Baudelaire: The oldest of the orphans, Violet is an inventor who pulls her hair out of her eyes when she is thinking. Symbols for Violet could include her namesake flower, hair ties, and inventions.

Klaus Baudelaire: Violet's brother is a voracious reader and researcher. His symbol would be a book.

Sunny Baudelaire: The baby of the orphan trio, Sunny has sharp little teeth and a vocabulary no one but her siblings can interpret. Symbols for her would include teeth and dentists.

VFD: Does it stand for Valorous Farms Dairy, the Vineyard of Fragrant Drapes, Veritable French Diner, Vain Fat Dictator, Violent Frozen Dragonflies, Vinegar Flavored Doughnuts, Very Fun Day, Very Fascinating Drama, or something else entirely? No one, with the possible exception of Daniel Handler, knows the answer, but the initials are used with greater frequency as the series develops. Be inventive and bend the clues around a VFD theme. (Very Filmy Dresses, Valuable Fire Department, etc.)

Clues and Stamp Ideas for A Series of Unfortunate Events

Book One: The Bad Beginning

Violet, Klaus, and Sunny Baudelaire are orphaned by a fire. Mr. Poe, their banker, places them with a distant cousin, Count Olaf, who plans to steal the Baudelaire fortune by marrying Violet, then killing all the siblings.

Clues and Stamps: Mansions, fire, banks, money, marriage, weddings.

Book Two: The Reptile Room

The Baudelaire children find brief happiness with herpetologist Dr. Montgomery, who plans to take them on a snake-finding expedition to Peru. Before that can happen, Dr. Montgomery is murdered by Count Olaf.

Clues and Stamps: Snakes, things that are snake-shaped, the letter "S," Peru.

Book Three: The Wide Window

The Baudelaire children live with Aunt Josephine Anwhistle in a house perched perilously on a cliff above Lake Lachrymose. Aunt Josephine fears everything except Count Olaf in a sailor disguise. Although the children try to save her by sailing across the lake in a hurricane, Aunt Josephine is eaten by Lake Lachrymose leeches.

Clues and Stamps: Lakes, houses perched on cliffs, aunts, sailors, pirates, clowns, sailboats, teardrops, leeches.

Book Four: The Miserable Mill

The orphans journey by train to Paltryville, where they are put to work debarking trees at the Lucky Smells Lumbermill. Klaus is hypnotized and almost commits murder by saw blade until his two siblings intervene.

Clues and Stamps: Trains, cigars, optical shops, chewing gum, lumber mill, saw blades, trees and tree bark, hypnotism.

Book Five: The Austere Academy

The orphans are sent to Prufrock Preparatory School, whose motto is "Memento Mori" ("Remember you will die"). They meet Isadora and Duncan Quagmire, whose parents and triplet brother died in a fire, leaving them sole heirs to the Quagmire sapphires. Count Olaf takes the Quagmires hostage and escapes in an airplane.

Clues and Stamps: Violins, bananas, cakes, measuring devices, S.O.R.E. (Special Orphans Running Exercises), airplanes, "Memento Mori," tombstones, sapphires.

Book Six: The Ersatz Elevator

The Baudelaire children are sent to live in the 71-bedroom penthouse home of Jerome and Esme Squalor, who live for daily reports of what is "in" and what is "out." Count Olaf, disguised as an auctioneer, is holding Isadora and Duncan Quagmire prisoner in an empty elevator shaft and later escapes by hiding them inside a red herring statue.

Clues and Stamps: Apartment buildings, "in" and "out," auctions, elevators, museums, bookstores, red herring, Very Fancy Doilies.

Book Seven: The Vile Village

The Baudelaires are housed with Hector in the Village of Fowl Devotees. They find evidence (Isadora's couplet poetry) that the Quagmires are nearby. The Baudelaires face being burned at the stake for the murder of a man who was found bitten to death. The Quagmires escape with Hector in his hot air balloon. Count Olaf escapes on a motorcycle. The Baudelaires, now identified as escaped murderers, gather remnants of the Quagmires' notebooks (containing evidence against Count Olaf) and flee.

Clues and Stamps: Crows, couplet poetry, hot air balloons, chores (trimming hedges, recycling, washing windows, polishing, making beds), hot fudge sundaes, town council, bread and water, jail, fountains, Daily Punctilio Newspaper, motorcycles, fowl.

Book Eight: The Hostile Hospital

The Baudelaire orphans take refuge in Heimlich Hospital, a half-finished institution manned by volunteers, where paperwork is of the utmost importance. Discovered by Count Olaf, who is disguised as the Head of Human Resources, Violet is scheduled for a cranioectomy (head removal) but is rescued by Klaus and Sunny after they solve an anagram using letters in alphabet soup.

Clues and Stamps: Hospitals, microphones, volunteers, fire, sugar bowls, files and file cabinets, hospital wards, nasty rashes, stubbed toes, Library of Records, Heimlich Maneuver, anagrams, alphabet soup, heads.

Book Nine: The Carnivorous Carnival

The Baudelaire orphans pose as carnival freaks in the Caligari Carnival until Count Olaf decides to feed the carnival lions a freak a day. They learn that volunteers all over the world are using VFD kits (veiled facial disguising, various finery disguises, and voice fakery disguises) in an attempt to bring Count Olaf to justice. Count Olaf kidnaps Sunny and heads for the Mortmain Mountains, where one of the Baudelaire parents might still be alive.

Clues and Stamps: Fortune tellers, crystal balls, wolf baby, corn, disguises, lions, roller coasters, circus caravan, maps, coffee stains, coded messages.

Book Ten: The Slippery Slope

Violet and Klaus meet the third Quagmire triplet, Quigley, who did not die in the fire that killed his parents. Eagles under the control of Count Olaf capture most of the book's characters in a net, but the Baudelaire children escape and now have information that the Count is headed for Hotel Denouement.

Clues and Stamps: Tea set, fire, snow, gnats, fencing masks, springpole (like a maypole), snow scouts, eagles, mountains, rivers, waterfalls, toboggans, nets, condiments.

Book Eleven: The Grim Grotto

The Baudelaires join Captain Widdershins aboard his submarine, the Queequeg, on a quest for an elusive sugar bowl. They nearly lose Sunny to poisonous mushrooms, then are held captive by Count Olaf and his henchmen before they escape to a mysterious rendezvous at Briny Beach.

Clues and Stamps: Submarines, sugar bowls, mushrooms, octopus, caves, poison, antidote, Briny Beach, taxis.

Letterboxing Party

Hold a party to celebrate the culmination of Letterboxing with Lemony Snicket. Collect the letterboxes and put the notebooks on display. Encourage participants to bring their own notebooks and stamps so they can stamp each other's books.

Invite participants to come in costume, as one of the Baudelaire or Quagmire orphans, Count Olaf, Lemony Snicket, or one of the other characters from the series.

Activities

VFD (Veiled Facial Disguising) Table

Recruit a volunteer to man a table where children can acquire face painting disguises and eye tattoos (painted or stamped) on their ankles.

Madame Lulu's Fortune Telling Table

Have a volunteer tell fortunes or read futures in a crystal ball.

Stamp Making

Even though the letterboxing activity is over, students may want to create and collect more personally designed stamps. Set aside an area and provide stamp-making materials.

Games

Very Foul Demise Game

Goal of the Game: The player designated as Count Olaf tries to murder his fellow players before his identity is revealed.

Play: Start by instructing all players to move around the room shaking hands with each other. The teacher or librarian joins the hand-shaking. While shaking hands she taps a finger three times quickly against one player's palm. That player is now Count Olaf. The teacher announces that Count Olaf is in the room. The hand-shaking continues, but now Count Olaf has the power to kill by tapping his finger three times on another player's palm while shaking hands. The doomed player should continue to shake hands with at least two, but no more than six, players before falling dead.

The remaining players cannot refuse to shake hands. If one of them thinks he knows who Count Olaf is, he can point at the suspect and say, "I accuse you of being the foul fiend, Count Olaf!" If he is right, the Count confesses, is captured, and the game is over. If the player's accusation is incorrect, the player making the accusation falls dead. When the number of players is reduced to two, Count Olaf is declared the winner. The next round of the game can be played with Count Olaf from the previous game choosing the new Count Olaf in the same way that the teacher or librarian did.

S.O.R.E. (Special Orphans Running Exercises)

Hold foot races, three-legged races, hopping races, and backward walking races. Give Austere Academy certificates as prizes.

Cakesniffing

Put fragrant items into paper lunch bags or plastic containers. Ask participants to close their eyes or wear a blindfold, sniff the contents of the bags, and guess which one is cake. Alternatively, players can guess the contents of every bag. Possible items: fresh rosemary, mint, cinnamon, pepper, or other herbs and spices; pine needles, rose petals, a cotton ball soaked in vinegar, rose-scented bath powder and, of course, cake.

Refreshments

Mount an all-lemon repast featuring lemon meringue pies and tarts, lemon pound cakes, lemon cookies, and bowls of lemon drop candies. Serve lemonade or sparkling lemonade made with equal parts of lemonade and seltzer, club soda, or tonic water. Keep the lemonade cool with a frozen lemonade ring into which lemon slices or violets have been frozen. (If using violets, arrange them carefully, upside down, on the bottom of a gelatin mold and cover with just enough lemonade to freeze them in place. After they are frozen, add liquid to the depth desired and return to the freezer.)

Alternatives to lemon overload could include cookies shaped, baked, and decorated to look like eyes, or snakes shaped from soft cheese spreads and covered with almond scales or slivers of red and green peppers.

Alternative beverages could include Lake Lachrymose Punch (lemon or limeade in which floats an ice ring containing gummy worms posing as Lake Lachrymose leeches). For a touch of sophistication, serve the Aqueous Martinis (water with an olive) described in *The Ersatz Elevator*.

Web Sites

The Series and Author

Foul Facts Gallery: Terrible Tudors, Vile Victorians, Social History
www.bbc.co.uk/history/society_culture/society/deary_gallery.shtml
British history written in the style of the series.

Fresh Air, National Public Radio
discover.npr.org/features/feature.jhtml?wfId=1143868
Interview with Daniel Handler.

KidsReads.com, A Series of Unfortunate Events
www.kidsreads.com/series/series-lemony-snicket-author.asp
A short bio of Lemony Snicket and four videos.

The Mysterious Mr. Snicket
www.salon.com/mwt/feature/2000/08/17/snicket/
An excellent, but PG13 level, interview with Daniel Hander.

Quidditch.com's Incomplete Guide to Lemony Snicket Allusions
www.quidditch.com/lemony%20snicket.htm
Interesting background about literary and social allusions in the books for teachers, librarians, and sophisticated students.

A Series of Unfortunate Events, Harper Collins
www.lemonysnicket.com/
The series Web site.

Letterboxing

Letterboxing North America WebRing
www.letterboxing.org/
Specific instructions for setting up letterboxes and creating individual stamps.

Stamp Making

Letterboxing Kids
www.letterboxing.org/kids/kids2.htm
Directions for making stamps with children.

Books in the Series

The Bad Beginning, Book One

The Reptile Room, Book the Second

The Wide Window, Book the Third

The Miserable Mill, Book the Fourth

The Austere Academy, Book the Fifth

The Ersatz Elevator, Book the Sixth

The Vile Village, Book the Seventh

The Hostile Hospital, Book the Eighth

The Carnivorous Carnival, Book the Ninth

The Slippery Slope, Book the Tenth

The Grim Grotto, Book the Eleventh

The Penultimate Peril, Book the Twelfth

All of the books in A Series of Unfortunate Events are available on HarperCollins audio tapes, read by Tim Curry. The tapes feature original music composed by Stephin Merritt and performed by his group, Gothic Archies, for which Lemony Snicket (Daniel Handler) plays the accordion.

Scholastic's Diary Series: My America, Dear America, My Name Is America

Authors: Susan Campbell Bartoletti, Marion Dane Bauer, Joseph Bruchac, Barry Denenberg, William Durbin, Lisa Rowe Fraustino, Sherry Garland, Kristiana Gregory, Joyce Hansen, Patricia Hermes, Karen Hesse, Sid Hite, Deborah Hopkinson Katelan Janke, Kathryn Lasky, Beth Seidel Levine, Ellen Levine, Megan McDonald, Patricia C. McKissack, Kate McMullan, Jim Murphy, Walter Dean Myers, Mary Pope Osborne, Rodman Philbrick, Ann Rinaldi, Ann Turner, Ellen Emerson White, Sharon Dennis Wyeth, Laurence Yep

• **Publisher:** Scholastic • **Age Levels:** My America, 6–8 years old; Dear America and My Name is America, 9–12 years old

Scholastic publishes four series of historical fiction for young readers based on a diary format: My America (featuring 7- to 12-year-old male and female protagonists), Dear America (featuring 12- to 18-year-old female protagonists), My Name is America (featuring 12- to 18-year-old male protagonists), and the Royal Diaries, which we will discuss in the next chapter. Books in the first three series, written by a variety of respected children's authors, tell historically accurate, optimistic stories about growing up in America during tumultuous and troubled times.

The diaries are an excellent curriculum adjunct for the study of both writing and history, and they are an equally wonderful springboard for a variety of Timeline Celebrations. Choose events based on seasons, holidays, or other important dates, or hold timeline dinners at any time of year, based on the time periods featured in the books.

Timeline Celebrations

Winter Holidays Timeline

Create a Winter Timeline Presentation as an alternative to a Winter Holiday play, where participants work in teams to research chosen moments in history and create corresponding holiday celebrations. (Teams could include parents or adult volunteers. If the times being researched fall during the twentieth century, team members might include participants who lived during those times.) Encourage participants to research how the protagonists in their books would have celebrated the winter holidays. What holiday would they have celebrated? What foods would they have eaten? How would they have decorated their houses? Would they have exchanged gifts? If so, what kinds of gifts? Did people exchange cards? What games and activities would they have engaged in? What kind of music would they have played or heard? What kind of clothes did they wear? Starting with the earliest date and progressing chronologically through time, have each group present the winter holiday celebration of its era.

Combine the Winter Holidays Timeline project with another holiday assembly or a Holiday Fair by having the participants set up timeline tables in the lobby, or give each group a classroom or space to decorate. Encourage participants in each group to dress in simple period costumes and act as historical re-enactors to the guests who time-travel between holiday celebrations. Era-appropriate refreshments might be available, either served by the students in each time period or at a timeline table in a central location. If gifts are a part of the group's holiday, consider giving inexpensive, token gifts to visitors.

The same project can be adapted to create timeline celebrations for other events, such as Thanksgiving/Harvest Home Feasts, Halloween, or weddings. See pages 58–59 for links to information about historical timelines and recipes.

Summer Timeline Picnic

Consider a Summer Timeline Picnic for an end-of-school-year event or a wrap-up event for a library summer reading program. Designate areas of a lawn, park, or playing field as different eras. Recruit volunteers to dress in period costume, act as historical re-enactors, and lead era-relevant games. Invite people to come in costume (though they are free to visit other time periods) and bring era-appropriate picnic lunches in suitable containers.

Food could also be provided or sold at a Food timeline table. Concentrate on easy to handle and eat foods, like hard cheeses, beef jerky, cornbread, and biscuits.

Games for Timeline Picnics

The games played during timeline picnics will depend on what games were popular during the eras you have chosen. Possibilities include Hide the Thimble, hoop racing, Quoits (horseshoes), Hopscotch, Jackstraws, Marbles, Tag, Jump Rope, and Capture the Flag. Check the Web sites section of this chapter for game possibilities and directions for playing them.

Election Day Timeline

Schools often function as precinct voting sites. If yours does, you are ideally situated to create an Election Day Timeline Event. Assign each group of participants a different presidential election year, or choose one election year and divide participants into two or more political

parties. Ask each party to research its candidate and the issues of that election. Parties can create campaign signs and literature and welcome voters by standing beside the school doors attired in roughly accurate period costume. Some participants might take up the women's suffrage cause, which spanned a number of elections.

If the school's Parent-Teacher Organization usually has an election-day bake sale, consider making at least part of it an Election Timeline Bake Sale. Offer johnny cake and dried apples from the colonial period, gingerbread and hardtack from the Civil War, Oreo cookies from 1912, Moon Pies from 1917, and original homemade Girl Scout cookies from 1922. (The recipe is available at the Girls Scouts of the United States of America Web site, listed on page 59.) Label each section of baked goods with the year of the election they represent.

Encourage participants to staff a History Polling Booth where voters can be invited to vote for the best and worst presidents in U.S. history, or the presidents they would most like to meet.

An announcement or story in the local newspaper would prepare voters for the students' project.

Timeline Dinners

Timeline Dinner Variation #1—The Timeline Fund-raising Dinner

Consider having a timeline dinner, or series of dinners, as a fund-raising alternative to the time-honored spaghetti dinner. For example, schedule a World War I Timeline Dinner sometime around Armistice Day (now known as Veteran's Day) in November. Directions for Slumpgullion, Bullets in a Pot, Fried Mush, Old Fashioned Doughnuts, and other recipes from *The Doughboy Cookbook*, are available online at worldwar1.com. An excellent food timeline with links to a multitude of recipes from a range of historical periods is available at the Morris County (NJ) Library Web site on page 59.

Timeline Dinner Variation #2—Timeline Potluck Dinner

Ask participants to bring a dish that represents a particular time in U.S. history. They can choose the time or it can be assigned, but make an attempt to span a range of years. Offer food suggestions if necessary. Cover the buffet table with a paper tablecloth, the edge of which has been decorated with a timeline. Note years only, or add major historical events. Arrange the potluck dishes in chronological order on the timeline tablecloth.

Decorations

Create a timeline along the wall by using a roll of brown craft paper or shelf paper. Divide it into sections and add significant events in world or United States history. Invite participants and guests to add their significant dates to the timeline (e.g., born, married, served in Vietnam, etc.) Alternatively, use paper tablecloths on which timelines have been drawn, inviting guests to add to their table's timeline, or invite guests to personalize paper place mats on which timelines have been drawn.

Create time capsule decorations for the tables by putting era-appropriate objects inside clear plastic Christmas ornaments or clear plastic boxes. Laminated copies of famous photos can be used as centerpieces. Time capsules and photos can also be suspended from the ceiling.

Entertainment for Timeline Dinners

What Do You Know?

Variation 1: Ask people in the school and community (perhaps local antique stores) to lend you objects like apple corers, skate keys, fon-due forks, and 45 rpm records. Number the objects and arrange them on tables. Provide paper and pencils and ask participants to guess the name and purpose of the items. Include objects that might be more recognizable to students than adults, like Yu-Gi-Oh cards and iPods.

Variation 2: Ask a local historical society or museum to bring odd and obscure items to a timeline event. Display an item, give participants enough time to write their guesses about its use on signed slips of paper, then collect the guesses. Display the next item while the slips are being examined for a winning guess.

Variation 3: Team Play.

<u>Preparation for the game:</u> Ask adult volunteers and students to collect objects they think people their age can identify but people of other ages might not. Create lists of trivia questions that meet the same criteria (e.g., "On the TV show *I Love Lucy* what was the name of Lucy's husband?" and "What is the name of Homer Simpson's wife?").

Create two-person teams. Team members can be any age but it is in a team's best interest to include a young person and an older person. Encourage grandchild-grandparent or teacher-student combinations. Assign someone the role of Game Show Host and someone else the role of scorekeeper.

<u>Play the game:</u> Send one member of the team out of the room. Ask the other member to identify objects and answer trivia questions. Score one point for every correct answer. Ask that player to predict whether her team member will be able to identify the objects and answer the questions. Bring the other member into the room. Ask the questions. Score one point for every correct answer and one additional point for answering the way his team member predicted. (Incorrect answers can result in points if the team member guessed he would not answer correctly.)

Use different sets of objects and questions for each team. When all the teams have had a turn, add up the points to determine the winning team. Alternatively, use the same objects and questions for everyone by having all members of all teams out of the room while the first half of the first team plays. Then call in the first half of the second team to play, then the first half of the third team, etc. When all first halves of the teams have answered, the second half of the first team is called in, followed by the second half of the second team, etc.

Timeline Dances

Timeline Dance Variation #1: Hold a dance that progresses through the dance styles popular throughout U.S. history. Start with the French minuet, English country dances, reels, hornpipes, jigs, and gavottes that were popular early in our country's history, then progress through the Charleston, Lindy Hop, Twist, Funky Chicken, and Disco Dancing to today's styles. Recruit someone to teach the simple basics of the dance steps. (Contredanses were a popular dance form in colonial times, so musicians and callers who lead today's contra dances might be able to teach some relatively authentic early dances. Dance teachers frequently teach the popular dances of the twentieth century and might be hired for an evening of group instruction. Older guests could teach the younger ones the dance steps of their day, and the younger guests could reciprocate by teaching their parents and grandparents how they dance now.) Move through the evening by moving the hands of a large clock, the numerals of which have been replaced by years, or by tearing the pages off a large calendar of years. Begin each new era by announcing the important news stories of the day. Live music is always wonderful, but recordings would work well, too.

Timeline Dance Variation #2: Choose one period of history and hold a dinner dance. Decorate, provide food and beverages, and include the music and dance styles of one of the following eras:

- Roaring Twenties (Charleston, Lindy Hop, Varsity Drag)

- Depression (Dance marathons)

- World War II (Swing)

- 1950s (Bossa Nova and Twist)

- 1960s (Hully-Gully, Watusi, Grapevine)

- 1970s (Disco)

- 1990s (Lambada, Macarena)

- 2000s (Hip-Hop, Breakdancing)

Web Sites

The Series and Authors

Dear America
www.scholastic.com/dearamerica/books/
Official Web site.

History

American Experience
www.pbs.org/wgbh/amex/
Historical information with links.

American Memory.com
memory.loc.gov/ammem/amhome.html
Links to more than 100 primary source collections.

Diaries, Memoirs, Letters, and Reports Along the Trails West
www.over-land.com/diaries.html
Links to diary excerpts.

eHistory.com
www.ehistory.com/world/timeline.cfm
Timelines and other historical information.

Eyewitness to History.com
www.eyewitnesstohistory.com/
Historical information from ancient times to the present time.

History Buff.com
www.historybuff.com/
Newspaper coverage of historical events.

History Central.com
www.multied.com/index.html
Includes links, timelines, wars, and elections.

NARA
www.archives.gov/index.html
Follow links for Digital Classroom to History in the Raw for discussion of diaries and primary sources.

The Net's Educational Resource Center
members.aol.com/TeacherNet/index.html
Links to a variety of history Web sites.

Time 100
www.time.com/time/time100/index.html
Short bios of *Time* magazine's 100 most influential people of the twentieth century.

Travilah Colonial America
www.mcps.k12.md.us/schools/travilahes/colonial.html
List of links for colonial America.

Christmas and Winter Holiday-Related Web sites

The Celebration of Christmas
www.motherbedford.com/Christmas.htm
Overview of Christmas, focusing on England and the early American colonies.

The History of Christmas
www.benbest.com/history/xmas.html
Overview of the holiday.

The Hymns and Carols of Christmas
www.hymnsandcarolsofchristmas.com/HTML/site_map.htm
History of Christmas cards, trees, and music.

Hanukkah, the Festival of Lights
www.factmonster.com/spot/hanukkah.html
Short history of Hanukkah traditions and food.

Happy Chanukah
www.holidays.net/chanukah/
History of Hanukkah.

Kwanzaa—A Celebration of Family, Community and Culture
www.officialkwanzaawebsite.org/
Official Web site of Kwanzaa.

Eid al Fitr, A Muslim Celebration
www.funsocialstudies.learninghaven.com/articles/eid.htm
History of Eid-al-Fitr.

Islam, Ramadan FAQ: Eid-al-Fitr
islam.about.com/library/weekly/aa121698j.htm
Links to information about Eid-al-Fitr and Ramadan.

Food

Civil War Recipes, Baked Goods
scnc.cps.k12.mi.us/baked_goods.htm

The Doughboy Cookbook
www.worldwar1.com/dbc/food.htm
Doughboy recipes from World War I.

Girl Scout Cookie History
www.girlscouts.org/about/cookie_hist.html
History of the Girl Scout cookie, including recipe.

History of Fashion, Food, and Time
members.aol.com/TeacherNet/FaFoTime.html
Links to wide range of clothing and food information, with recipes.

Morris County Library's Food Timeline
www.foodtimeline.org
Food timeline with links to recipes and resources.

Music and Dance

American Music Timeline
www.infoplease.com/spot/musictime1.html
Timeline with brief descriptions.

ClassicalWorks Timeline
www.classicalworks.com/his.pages/timeline.html
Timeline of classical music.

Dance History Archives
www.streetswing.com/histmain/d5timlne.htm
Dance history timeline.

Music Timeline
www.infoplease.com/ipea/A0151192.html
Timeline with brief descriptions of popular musical styles.

Games

Colonial Games and Toys
noahwebsterhouse.org/games.html
Toys, games, nursery rhymes, and riddles of colonial America.

Games Kids Play, Geof Nieboer
www.gameskidsplay.net/
Children's games and their rules.

Kids Games
www.everyrule.com/kids_azlist.html
Listing of rules for a wide range of kids' games.

The Online Guide to Traditional Games, History and Useful Information
www.tradgames.org.uk/index.html
List of traditional board, lawn, and pub games.

Books in Scholastic's Diary Series

My America

Colonial Period, 1600s to 1700s

Our Strange New Land: Elizabeth's Diary, Jamestown, Virginia, 1609 by Patricia Hermes

The Starving Time: Elizabeth's Diary; Book Two, Jamestown, Virginia, 1609 by Patricia Hermes

Season of Promise: Elizabeth's Jamestown Colony Diary; Book Three, Jamestown, Virginia, 1611 by Patricia Hermes

American Revolution, 1700s

Five Smooth Stones: Hope's Diary, Philadelphia, Pennsylvania, 1776 by Kristiana Gregory

We Are Patriots: Hope's Revolutionary War Diary, Book Two, Valley Forge, Pennsylvania, 1777 by Kristiana Gregory

When Freedom Comes: Hope's Revolutionary War Diary, Book Three, 1778 by Kristiana Gregory

Westward Expansion, 1800s

Westward to Home: Joshua's Diary, Book One, The Oregon Trail, 1848 by Patricia Hermes

A Perfect Place: Joshua's Oregon Trail Diary, Book Two, 1848 by Patricia Hermes

The Wild Year: Joshua's Oregon Trail Diary, Book Three, 1849 by Patricia Hermes

As Far As I Can See: Meg's Prairie Diary, St. Louis to the Kansas Territory, 1856 by Kate McMullan

For This Land: Meg's Prairie Diary, Book Two, 1856 by Kate McMullan

A Fine start: Meg's Prairie Diary, Book Three, 1857 by Kate McMullan

Underground Railroad, 1850s to 1860s

Freedom's Wings: Corey's Diary, Kentucky to Ohio, 1857 by Sharon Dennis Wyeth

Flying Free: Corey's Underground Railroad Diary, Book Two, Amherstburg, Canada, 1858 by Sharon Dennis Wyeth

Message in the Sky: Corey's Underground Railroad Diary, Book Three, 1859 by Sharon Dennis Wyeth

Civil War/Slavery 1850s to 1870s

My Brother's Keeper: Virginia's Civil War Diary, Book One, Gettysburg, PA, 1863 by Mary Pope Osborne

After the Rain: Virginia's Civil War Diary, Book Two, Washington, D.C., 1864 by Mary Pope Osborne

A Time to Dance: Virginia's Civil War Diary, Book Three, 1865–1866 by Mary Pope Osborne

Twentieth Century Immigration

Hope in My Heart: Sofia's Immigrant Diary, Book One, 1903 by Kathryn Lasky

Home at Last: Sofia's Immigrant Diary, Book Two, 1903 by Kathryn Lasky

An American Spring: Sofia's Immigrant Diary, Book Three, 1903 by Kathryn Lasky

Dear America

Colonial Period, 1600s to 1700s

A Journey to the New World: The Diary of Remember Patience Whipple, Mayflower, 1620 by Kathryn Lasky

I Walk in Dread: The Diary of Deliverance Trembly, Witness to the Salem Witch Trials, Massachusetts Bay Colony, 1691 by Lisa Rowe Fraustino

Standing in the Light: The Captive Diary of Catharine Carey Logan, Delaware Valley, Pennsylvania, 1763 by Mary Pope Osborne

Look to the Hills: The Diary of Lozette Maoreau, a French Slave Girl, New York Colony, 1763 by Patricia McKissack

American Revolution, 1770s

The Winter of Red Snow: The Revolutionary War Diary of Abigail Jane Stewart, Valley Forge, Pennsylvania, 1777 by Kristiana Gregory

Love Thy Neighbor: the Tory Diary of Prudence Emerson, Greenmarsh, Massachusetts, 1774 by Ann Turner

Westward Expansion, 1800s

A Line in the Sand: The Alamo Diary of Lucinda Lawrence, Gonzales, Texas, 1836 by Sherry Garland

Valley of the Moon: The Diary of Maria Rosalia de Milagros, Sonoma Valley, Alta California, 1846 by Sherry Garland

Across the Wide and Lonesome Prairie: The Oregon Trail Diary of Hattie Campbell, 1847 by Kristiana Gregory

All the Stars in the Sky: The Santa Fe Trail Diary of Florrie Mack Ryder, The Sante Fe Trail, 1848 by Megan McDonald

Seeds of Hope: The Gold Rush Diary of Susanna Fairchild, California Territory, 1849 by Kristiana Gregory

The Great Railroad Race: The Diary of Libby West, Utah Territory, 1868 by Kristiana Gregory

My Face to the Wind: The Diary of Sarah Jane Price, A Prairie Teacher, Broken Bow, Nebraska, 1881 by Jim Murphy

West to a Land of Plenty: The Diary of Teresa Angelino Viscardi, New York to Idaho Territory, 1883 by Jim Murphy

Land of the Buffalo Bones: The Diary of Mary Elizabeth Rodgers, An English Girl in Minnesota, New Yeovil, Minnesota, 1873 by Marion Dane Bauer

Civil War/Slavery, 1850s to 1870s

A Picture of Freedom: The Diary of Clotee, A Slave Girl, Belmont Plantation, Virginia, 1859 by Patricia McKissack

A Light in the Storm: The Civil War Diary of Amelia Martin, Fenwick Island, Delaware, 1861 by Karen Hesse

When Will This Cruel War Be Over? The Civil War Diary of Emma Simpson, Gordonsville, Virginia, 1864 by Barry Denenberg

I Thought My Soul Would Rise and Fly: The Diary of Patsy, a Freed Girl, Mars Bluff, South Carolina, 1865 by Joyce Hansen

Nineteenth Century Immigration, 1800s

So Far From Home: The Diary of Mary Driscoll, an Irish Mill Girl, Lowell, Massachusetts, 1847 by Barry Denenberg

A Coal Miner's Bride: The Diary of Anetka Kaminska, Lattimer, Pennsylvania, 1896 by Susan Campbell Bartoletti

Native American Experience, late 1800s

The Girl Who Chased Away Sorrow: The Diary of Sarah Nita, a Navajo Girl, New Mexico, 1864 by Ann Turner

My Heart is on the Ground: The Diary of Nannie Little Rose, a Sioux Girl, Carlisle Indian School, Pennsylvania, 1880 by Ann Rinaldi

Twentieth Century Immigration, 1900s

Dreams in the Golden Country: The Diary of Zipporah Feldman, a Jewish Immigrant Girl, New York City, 1903 by Kathryn Lasky

Early Twentieth Century, 1900 to 1930s

Hear My Sorrow: The Diary of Angela Denoto, a Shirtwaist Worker, New York City, 1909 by Deborah Hopkinson

Voyage on the Great Titanic: The Diary of Margaret Ann Brady, R.M.S. Titanic, 1912 by Ellen Emerson White

Color Me Dark: The Diary of Nellie Lee Love, the Great Migration North, Chicago, Illinois, 1919 by Patricia McKissack

World War I, 1910s to 1920s

A Time for Courage: The Suffragette Diary of Kathleen Bowen, Washington, D.C., 1917 by Kathryn Lasky

When Christmas Comes Again: The World War I Diary of Simone Spencer, New York City to the Western Front, 1917 by Beth Seidel Levine

The Depression, 1930s

Christmas After All: The Great Depression Diary of Minnie Swift, Indianapolis, IN, 1932 by Kathryn Lasky

Mirror, Mirror on the Wall: The Diary of Bess Brennan, The Perkins School for the Blind, Watertown, MA, 1932 by Barry Denenberg

Survival in the Storm: The Dust Bowl Diary of Grace Edwards, Dalhart, Texas, 1935 by Katelan Janke

World War II, 1930s to 1940s

One Eye Laughing, The Other Weeping: The Diary of Julie Weiss, Vienna, Austria, to New York, 1938 by Barry Denenberg

My Secret War: The World War II Diary of Madeline Beck, Long Island, New York, 1941 by Mary Pope Osborne

Early Sunday Morning: The Pearl Harbor Diary of Amber Billows, Hawaii, 1941 by Barry Denenberg

Vietnam, 1960s to 1970s

Where Have All the Flowers Gone? The Diary of Molly MacKenzie Flaherty, Boston, Massachusetts, 1968 by Ellen Emerson White

My Name Is America

Colonial Period, 1600s–1700s

The Journal of Jasper Jonathan Pierce: A Pilgrim Boy, Plymouth, 1620 by Ann Rinaldi

American Revolution, 1770s

The Journal of William Thomas Emerson: A Revolutionary War Patriot, Boston, Massachusetts, 1774 by Barry Denenberg

Westward Expansion, 1800s

The Journal of Augustus Pelletier: The Lewis and Clark Expedition, 1804 by Kathryn Lasky

The Journal of Jedediah Barstow: An Emigrant on the Oregon Trail, Overland, 1845 by Ellen Levine

The Journal of Douglas Allen Deeds: The Donner Party Expedition, 1846 by Rodman Philbrick

The Journal of Wong Ming-Chung: A Chinese Miner, California, 1852 by Laurence Yep

The Journal of Sean Sullivan: A Transcontinental Railroad Worker, Nebraska and Points West, 1867 by William Durbin

The Journal of Joshua Loper: A Black Cowboy, the Chisholm Trail, 1871 by Walter Dean Myers

The Journal of Brian Doyle: A Greenhorn on an Alaskan Whaling Ship, 1874 by Jim Murphy

Civil War/Slavery, 1850s–1870s

The Journal of Rufus Rowe: A Witness to the Battle of Fredricksburg, Bowling Green, Virginia, 1862 by Sid Hite

The Journal of James Edmund Pease: A Civil War Union Soldier, Virginia, 1863 by Jim Murphy

Native American Experience, late 1800s

The Journal of Jesse Smoke: A Cherokee Boy, The Trail of Tears, 1838 by Joseph Bruchac

Twentieth Century Immigration:

The Journal of Finn Reardon: A Newsie, New York City, 1899 by Susan Campbell Bartoletti

The Journal of Otto Peltonen: A Finnish Immigrant, Hibbing, Minnesota, 1905 by William Durbin

The Depression, 1930s

The Journal of C. J. Jackson: A Dust Bowl Migrant, Oklahoma to California, 1935 by William Durbin

World War II, 1930s to 1940s

The Journal of Ben Uchida: Citizen 13559, Mirror Lake Internment Camp, California, 1942 by Barry Denenberg

The Journal of Scott Pendleton Collins: A World War II Soldier, Normandy, France, 1944 by Walter Dean Myers

Civil Rights, 1940s to 1950s

The Journal of Biddy Owens: The Negro Leagues, Birmingham, Alabama, 1948 by Walter Dean Myers

Vietnam War, 1960s to 1970s

The Journal of Patrick Seamus Flaherty: United States Marine Corps, Khe Sanh, Vietnam, 1968 by Ellen Emerson White

The Royal Diaries

Authors: Barry Denenberg, Kristiana Gregory, Sheri Holman, Anna Kirwan, Kathryn Lasky, Patricia C. McKissack, Carolyn Meyer, Patricia Clark Smith, Ellen Emerson White, Laurence Yep • **Publisher:** Scholastic • **Age Level:** 9–12 years old

The Royal Diaries series follows the same format as Scholastic's three diary series discussed in the previous chapter, but the books go much farther afield geographically and culturally. Drawing on the history of young women born into royal families, the books examine the difficulty of growing up in the dangerous environment that power often creates.

The Royal Diaries are not about affluence and extravagance. They are about responsibility, trust, betrayal, and political intrigue. Give students a taste of danger by staging a Royal Diaries Power Lunch, during which participants play Court Intrigue.

The Royal Diaries Power Lunch

The Royal Diaries Power Lunch can take place within a classroom or with several classes combined. It can be limited to one age group, or it can be expanded to include administrators, teachers, custodians, school secretaries, and parents. Distribute copies of the instructions for Court Intrigue to all participants prior to the day of the Power Lunch to give players a chance to absorb the details and think about strategy.

Goal of the Game

For students in the roles of Prince or Princess, the goal of Court Intrigue is to be the ruling monarch at the end of the game. For everyone else, the goal is to be allied with the winning royal and to make as much profit from that alliance as possible.

Assign roles and wealth to participants as they arrive for the Power Lunch (see Court Intrigue instructions), then encourage people to move around the room, talking, gathering information, making deals, and plotting while they eat. When the food has been consumed, move on to the decision-making part of Court Intrigue.

Food

The most important quality of the food served at the Royal Diaries Power Lunch is that the dishes encourage participants to gather in small groups. Place plates of the following foods around the room:

- crackers with cheese, pâtés, or spreads
- chips and dips
- deviled eggs
- celery stalks filled with cream cheese or peanut butter, sprinkled with raisins
- vegetable crudités with dips (dips can be as simple as blue cheese or ranch dressing)
- fruit slices with dips (lemon yogurt, fruit yogurt, or sour cream sweetened to taste with brown sugar, cinnamon, and nutmeg)
- peanuts in the shell
- vanilla wafer cookies or small slices of pound cake with spreads (jam or chocolate pudding)

Beverages

Serve raspberry ginger ale in plastic champagne glasses, decorated with toothpick skewers of cherries, strawberries, melon, and pineapple chunks and mugs of ginger ale or root beer.

The Game of Court Intrigue

Preparation

Make as many birthright bags (paper bags or cloth sacks) as there will be players. Put a title into each bag. (For example, prince/princess, duke/duchess, count/countess, baron/baroness, viscount/viscountess, marquis/marchioness—the gender of the role will be determined by the gender of the participant. The title might be on a name tag the player can wear.) There can be many dukes, counts, barons, viscounts, marquises, and their female counterparts, but there can be only two royal heirs (prince/princess). Put 10 to 20 pieces of gold in each bag. (The pieces of gold can be pennies, pieces of cardboard, poker chips, or other tokens.) There need not be an equal number of tokens in each bag. Put all of the birthright bags into a larger container and ask participants to reach into the container to select a bag that will represent their title and wealth. When the princes or princesses have been identified, give each of them an additional bag of tokens equal to 10 tokens for every other participant in the game.

How to Play

While participants move about the room chatting and eating, the two royals should be consolidating their power by making promises and deals. They want every player to promise to back their claim to the throne later in the game. They can give members of the court money, or promise to give them money after they come to power. Members of the court make deals and promises as well. Promises may or may not be kept later.

When the eating and chatting part of the Power Lunch is finished, it is time to choose a sovereign. The two opposing royals stand on opposite sides of the room and call their courts to gather around them. Players move to one side of the room or the other to reveal their loyalties. The royal with the greatest number of followers is crowned King or Queen. Courtiers who were loyal to the losing royal forfeit half of their wealth to the newly-crowned monarch. Players who supported the winning monarch may be rewarded, as the monarch sees fit, out of the forfeited possessions of the losing players. The losing royal keeps his property unless he or she is executed (see Option 4).

In the simplest version of the game, the royal with the largest number of followers is crowned monarch. His or her followers are rewarded, and the game ends. The game can be made more complicated by adding the following options:

Option 1: Followers of the reigning monarch can change their minds. If the distribution of confiscated property (which is entirely at the discretion of the monarch) does not please a follower, he can cross the room and join the losing side. Half of his property will be forfeited to the reigning monarch, but he may be able to get a reward from the losing royal. If enough followers join the losing royal to give him a majority, he becomes the new monarch, takes half of the possessions from everyone still loyal to the old monarch, and redistributes them as he sees fit. The newly deposed monarch keeps her wealth.

Option 2: A monarch can banish a follower from her court, taking half of that person's wealth when he goes. She might do this if she thinks the player has a large amount of wealth she can confiscate. It is to the monarch's financial advantage to have as many people on the losing side as possible in order to maximize the amount of forfeited property, but it is a risky strategy. Having only a few more followers than her rival puts her at risk of losing the throne if any of her followers defect to the other royal's court.

Option 3: A winning royal can invite followers of the losing royal to be part of her court. She may offer a reward or simply safety in case something happens to the losing royal. The reason she would offer a reward or sanctuary to those who were not loyal to her in the beginning will become clear with the next option.

Option 4: The winning royal can murder her rival, thereby removing the possibility that followers can change sides and force her into the losing position. However, regicide is not easy. She may murder her rival only if her rival has only one follower left on his side. (Adjust this number to two or three followers if playing with a large group of people.) The murderous monarch must state her intentions by pointing at her rival and declaring, "Treason!"

Followers of the reigning monarch may choose to change sides, thereby increasing the number of protectors to the minimum needed to prevent regicide. (Why would a player move from the winning court to the losing court to protect an imperiled royal? See Option 5.)

If no one from the ruling monarch's side moves to the defense of the other royal, the Monarch declares "Execution!" The losing royal and his follower(s) are executed. All property, including that of the executed royal, is forfeited to the reigning monarch.

Option 5: When the losing royal is dead, the ruling monarch becomes immensely powerful. No one can stop her because there is no other court to join. She can do whatever she wishes, including confiscating property from all the other players, exiling them, or having them executed. It is actually in the players' best interests to make sure both monarchs remain alive.

Option 6: A member of the court may challenge the ruling monarch and take her throne if he has more money than the monarch. He can accrue the money himself by making deals with the monarch while she squanders her money away, or he can convince other players to give him their money, perhaps by promising to return it with interest when he becomes the reigning monarch.

The usurper mounts a challenge by pointing at the monarch and declaring, "Revolution!" He displays his wealth. She displays hers. Other players may give her money so that she has enough wealth to block the takeover.

If the challenger wins, he is crowned monarch. The defeated monarch forfeits half of her wealth to the new monarch and may choose to stay in the court or join her royal counterpart in the other court.

If the challenger loses, he is executed for treason and his wealth is forfeited to the monarch.

Money given to the challenger or to the monarch during a revolution is the property of the challenger or monarch. It need not be returned. Promises to do so may or may not be kept.

The End

The game ends when no more action is possible (when one monarch's power is so absolute, no action other than her orders can be taken) or when the time allotted for the Royal Diaries Power Lunch has come to an end. If the game is called for time, the situation is as it is. That is, players are in the court of the winning or losing royal, and they have whatever wealth they have.

Books in the Royal Diaries Series

Cleopatra VII: Daughter of the Nile, Egypt, 57 BC by Kristiana Gregory

Lady of Cha'Iao Kuo: Warrior of the South, Southern China, AD 531 by Laurence Yep

Sondok: Princess of the Moon and Stars, Korea, AD 595 by Sheri Holman

Lady of Palenque: Flower of Bacal, Mesoamerica, AD 749 by Anna Kirwan

Eleanor: Crown Jewel of Aquitaine, France, 1136 by Kristiana Gregory

Isabel: Jewel of Castilla, Spain, 1466 by Carolyn Meyer

Elizabeth I: Red Rose of the House of Tudor, England, 1544 by Kathryn Lasky

Mary Queen of Scots: Queen Without a Country, France, 1553 by Kathryn Lasky

Nzingha: Warrior Queen of Matamba, Angola, Africa, 1595 by Patricia McKissack

Jahanara: Princess of Princesses, India, 1627 by Kathryn Lasky

Kristina: The Girl King, Sweden, 1638 by Carolyn Meyer

Weetamoo: Heart of the Pocassets, Massachusetts-Rhode Island, 1653 by Patricia Clark Smith

Marie Antoinette: Princess of Versailles, Austria-France, 1769 by Kathryn Lasky

Victoria: May Blossom of Britannia, England, 1829 by Anna Kirwan

Elisabeth of Austria: The Princess Bride, 1853 by Barry Denenberg

Kazunomiya: Prisoner of Heaven, Japan, 1858 by Kathryn Lasky

Kaiulani: The People's Princess, Hawaii, 1889 by Ellen Emerson White

Anastasia: The Last Grand Duchess, Russia, 1914 by Carolyn Meyer

Harry Potter

Author: J. K. Rowling • **Illustrator:** Mary GrandPré • **Publisher:** Scholastic
Age Level: 10 years old to young adult

The reigning masterpiece of contemporary children's fantasy literature, the Harry Potter saga starts with a long-suffering orphan discovering that he is someone special—a wizard who, as a child, was the only creature ever to thwart the will of evil Lord Voldemort. Each novel in the series spans a year in the life of Harry Potter and his friends, foes, and teachers at Hogwarts School of Witchcraft and Wizardry. As he grows older, Harry faces a growing threat from a steadily rejuvenated and alarmingly more powerful Voldemort.

The Harry Potter series weaves together the classic themes of children's literature, most notably the search for family, friendship, and a sense of belonging, and the battle between good and evil, both outside and inside oneself. But the genius of the Harry Potter books lies in J. K. Rowling's copious details of the magic world. It is these details that make the Harry Potter books so much fun to read and so easy to use in a literary celebration like Diagon Alley Day.

Diagon Alley Day

Diagon Alley Day can be a classroom-contained activity or a school-wide celebration. It could also be used as a school or library fund-raising event.

Turn your school or library into Diagon Alley, the wizard-world's version of a shopping and business district, complete with the following wizard businesses:

Gringott's Bank

Exchange muggle money for wizard-world money that can be used to make purchases in Diagon Alley.

Wizard-World Currency

Design a system of currency for the wizard world based on the following specifications from the Harry Potter books:

Galleon: (Unum Galleon) Made of Gold, worth 17 Sickles or 493 Knuts.

Sickle: (Unum Sickle) Made of silver, worth 29 Knuts.

Knut: (Unum Knut) Made of copper.

Create designs and colors for the denominations of wizard money, keeping in mind that the designs must conform to the method by which the money will be reproduced. That is, paper bills that will be printed by running colored paper through a copy machine will have to be a single color with black print unless you have access to a color copier. Make coins by gluing paper circles to poker chips or cardboard discs.

Establish a Gringott's Bank table at which U.S. currency can be exchanged for wizard-world currency as people enter Diagon Alley and converted back to U.S. currency as they leave.

CNN Money's currency conversion Web site has calculated the relative value of U.S. currency and wizard-world currency as follows:

Wizard-world	U.S. Currency
1 galleon	$4.82
1 sickle	28 cents
1 knut	1 cent
$1.00	3 sickles and 15 knuts
75 cents	2 sickles and 19 knuts

1 sickle and 22 knuts	50 cents
26 knuts	25 cents
10 knuts	10 cents
5 knuts	5 cents
1 knut	1 cent

Flourish & Blott's

In addition to selling used books, set aside a Preview-of-Hogwarts area for a potions class. Recruit a student or adult volunteer to be the potions teacher. See the potions section on pages 70–71 for possible brews.

Madame Malkin's Robes for all Occasions

Encourage Diagon Alley Day participants to arrive in costume. For those who have left their wizard world wardrobe at home, provide robes and other appropriate attire. The clothing can be loaned, rented, or offered for sale.

Recruit a volunteer to help participants make witch and wizard hats.

Wizard Hats

Start with a 17" x 17" square of paper. Use a pair of scissors to round one corner of the square. Decorate the surface of the hat with paint, markers, or stickers. Roll the paper so that the straight sides overlap slightly and the paper forms a cone. Tape the hat together along the straight seam. If necessary, trim the bottom edge of the hat to make it even. For ties, cut two 12" pieces of ribbon or yarn. Tape one end of each ribbon to the inside of the hat, or punch holes in each side of the hat with a paper punch, insert the ribbon, and tie a loose knot.

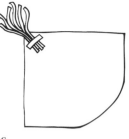

To make the hat more decorative, tape the end of a length of lightweight cloth, crepe paper streamers, or metallic shreds inside the point of the hat. The streamers should be positioned so they emerge from the point of the hat after it is rolled into a cone.

Ollivanders

Makers of fine wands since 382 BC. Recruit a volunteer to help participants make magic wands.

Magic Wands

Lay a 12" long wooden dowel (or two unsharpened pencils taped together end to end) on a piece of metallic foil 1" wide and slightly longer than the dowel. Make a 12" long bundle of foil strips, curled ribbon, colored paper shreds, or metallic star garlands. Fasten a twist tie or pipe cleaner around the end of the bundle, then use the ends of the twist tie to fasten the bundle to the dowel. Roll the foil around the dowel and tape it in place.

Quality Quidditch Supplies

Everyone who has read the Harry Potter books knows about quidditch—the broomstick-riding, bludger-avoiding, snitch-seeking sensation of the wizard sports world. If you have access to a gymnasium or playing field, consider staging a game of Muggle Quidditch (ground quidditch for non-magical players). See the Web sites on page 73 for instructions.

In addition to schedules of quidditch matches, Quality Quidditch Supplies would supply banners and posters of favorite teams. Provide a table with paper and markers or felt pieces and glue for participants to make banners and posters for the teams associated with each Hogwarts house (Gryffindor, Ravenclaw, Hufflepuff, and Slytherin), or for major league Quidditch teams, like Ron's favorite, the Chudley Cannons. (See the Web Site list on page 73 for Quidditch information.)

Gambol and Japes Wizarding Joke Shop

Gambol and Japes could serve as the venue for a demonstration of magic by an adult or student volunteer. It could host a Magic Workshop, during which older students and adults could teach some basic magic tricks to interested novices. Or there could be a Joke and Tricks open-mike event, during which amateur magicians each take turns performing.

Set up a table at which participants can write messages with Fred and George Weasley's Disappearing Ink (lemon juice applied to paper with fine-tipped paintbrushes or Q-tips). Have a light bulb or toaster nearby to show how the message magically reappears when subjected to the light of knowledge or the heat of passion.

If Diagon Alley Day is a fund-raiser, consider selling small joke items purchased online or at a discount store.

Magical Menagerie

Recruit a volunteer to help participants create origami toads, owls, and other creatures. (See the Web sites on page 73.)

Provide materials (paper and markers, recycled materials, and glue, clay, and paint) participants can use to create magical creatures.

Arrange a demonstration of snakes, toads, owls, or other creatures by a pet owner or a representative from a local Audubon Society chapter or zoo.

Ministry of Magic

The Ministry of Magic is the perfect place for a Muggle Artifact Sale (known in the muggle world as a White Elephant Sale).

Borgin and Burkes

Mr. Borgin's shop is not on Diagon Alley. It is nearby, on the totally disreputable Knockturn Alley. For a small fee, participants could see a display of very disturbing objects in this shop devoted to the dark arts.

Borgin & Burkes's Disturbing Inventory

Raw Egg without a Shell: Put a raw egg into a glass jar with a lid. Pour in enough white vinegar to cover the egg. Wait five days. The shell will dissolve, leaving the raw egg encased in an egg-shaped membrane. (If the jar is small, there may not be enough vinegar to complete the decalcification process. If that is the case, replace the old vinegar with fresh vinegar after two or three days.) To display the egg, pour off the vinegar and leave the jar open so the egg can be (carefully) touched.

Bendable Chicken Bone: Place a chicken leg bone in a jar with a lid. (A bone from a cooked chicken works fine.) Fill the jar with white vinegar. In about a week the bone can be removed from the vinegar and bent.

A Boneless Hand: Fill a good quality, but not too thick, rubber glove with cooked oatmeal. Tie it securely shut. Slide it into the sleeve of a jacket or sweater and use small safety pins to secure it to the inside of the sleeve. (Be sure to use the safety pins above the knot, not on the part of the glove that contains the oatmeal.) Leave the jacket with hand on a display table. Alternatively, hold the glove, pull the sleeve of your jacket down to hide your own hand, and offer the boneless hand in handshakes.

Anything in a Glass Jar: Almost anything looks horrifying in a glass jar filled with water, especially if the water is murky (like mop water). Try coiled rubber snakes, plastic bugs and lizards, and old doll's heads.

Supermarket Horrors: Visit the meat counter of your local supermarket for items that look ghastly even when they aren't floating in a glass jar of white vinegar or alcohol. We suggest beef tongue, heart, and kidneys, and a nice bouquet of chicken feet. Talk to the butcher ahead of time to secure the very best of horrors.

Food Samples: Fill paper pill cups with sample dark arts snacks like locally-grown Organic Maggots (cooked white rice), Imported Tasmanian Maggots (cooked brown rice), Jumbo Fresh Water Maggots (cooked macaroni), and Giant Green Spider Eyeballs (peeled green grapes).

Honeydukes

Technically, Honeydukes Sweetshop is located in the village of Hogsmeade, but for the purpose of this celebration, it has opened a branch in Diagon Alley. For Honeydukes inventory, use penny candy, renamed with magical names, or have volunteers create and package their own Honeydukes treats. Honeydukes is especially renowned for its fudge and chocolate.

Set aside a table at Honeydukes for the creation of Wizard Cards (the kind Ron and Harry find in packages of chocolate frogs). Provide pencils, markers, pre-cut poster board rectangles, and sheets of wizard card backs and fronts. (The backs are covered with a fanciful design. The fronts look like frames. The backs and fronts are the same size as the pre-cut poster board rectangles.) When participants have colored the cards and drawn portraits of their favorite witches and wizards inside the frames, have them cut out the cards and paste them to the poster board rectangles.

Florian Fortescue's Ice Cream Parlor

Sell ice cream and/or make-your-own sundaes. See the Recipes section of this chapter for recipes for Florian Fortescue's Celestial Ices, Hot Blood Sundaes, and Quaffle Waffle Quidditch Sundaes.

The Leaky Cauldron

Create a tavern where customers can order butter beer and pumpkin juice. (See the Recipes and Web site sections.)

Street Vendors and Activities

Fill Diagon Alley with any, or all, of the following:

- Costumes and props: Encourage participants and guests to come attired in old graduation gowns, choir robes, witchy-looking dresses, batty hats, and handbags that could hold an owl or a dragon's egg.

- A fencing demonstration or student fencing with nerf swords.

- Professional, amateur, or student magicians and jugglers.

- A face-painting booth that specializes in lightning bolts.

- Hogwarts Parent-Teacher Association Bake Sale: A food table with wizard world and muggle food items.

- Palm readers, crystal ball gazers, and tea leaf readers.

- Ghost Storytellers: Recruit a volunteer to dress as Nearly Headless Nick or one of Hogwart's other ghostly residents. He can tell stories about the ghosts he has known or simply wander through Diagon Alley greeting guests with a cheery "Hi-ho!"

Potions

Professor McGonigal's Transformation Slime

Combine one cup of water with one tablespoon of Borax. In a separate bowl, combine three tablespoons of white glue with two tablespoons of water. Stir both solutions until thoroughly mixed. Put three tablespoons of the glue mixture into a plastic bag with a zip closing. Add three drops of food coloring and one tablespoon of the Borax mixture to the bag. Zip the bag shut and work the mixture with your fingers until it begins to form a solid. Remove the solid substance from the bag and work it with your hands. The mixture can be used like Silly Putty to make prints from newspaper comics. Store it in the refrigerator when not in use.

Professor Snape's Solid to Liquid Transmogrifying Potion

Place ½ cup of cornstarch in a small bowl. Add six to eight tablespoons of water, one tablespoon at a time, until the cornstarch looks liquid. (Add the last two tablespoons slowly. You may not need all of the water.) Pick the potion up in your hands. It alternates between being a solid and a liquid.

Moaning Myrtle's Toilet Water

In a small jar, combine ¼ cup of witch hazel and 1½ teaspoons of glycerine. (Available in drugstores, often mixed with rose water.) Add ¼ cup strongly-brewed, cooled herbal lemon tea, and ½ teaspoon lemon extract. Close the jar and shake well. This mixture makes a pleasant after-bath splash.

Recipes

Blood Oranges

Serve alone or on a slice of pound cake with an orange sauce. (Orange marmalade thinned to desired consistency with orange juice, heated slightly in a microwave or double boiler.)

Bertie Bott's Every Flavor Bean

Use regular jelly beans or purchase Bertie Bott's Every Flavor Beans online or at a candy store.

Quaffle Waffles

Italian waffle cookies, also known as pizzelles, can be purchased in supermarkets. Top with a scoop of lemon sherbet ice cream and decorate with lemon half-slice wings to make a Quaffle Waffle Quidditch Sundae.

Florian Fortescue's Celestial Ice

Make frozen ices shaped like heavenly bodies by freezing fruit juice in star- and moon-shaped molds available at craft stores.

Madame Pomfrey's Wonderful Wand Dip

Stir colored sprinkles into white cake frosting. Serve with breadsticks, pretzels, or goldfish for dipping.

Magic Wands

Melt chocolate, white chocolate, or butterscotch chips in a double boiler or microwave oven. Dip pretzel sticks halfway up their length into the chocolate, then roll them in sugar sparkles or colored sprinkles. Allow them to dry on a sheet of waxed paper or standing upright in a glass.

Edible Bones

Melt white chocolate in a double boiler or microwave oven. Dip pretzel sticks halfway up their lengths in the chocolate. Allow them to cool. Dip the other end of the pretzel into the white chocolate to cover the entire stick. Allow them to cool.

Blast-ended Skrewt Treats

Decorate the rims of ice cream cones by pressing them into cake frosting or piping a line of frosting along the rims, then pressing the rims into colored sprinkles or sugar sparkles. Fill the cones with colorful cereal.

Hot Blood Sundaes

Drizzle vanilla ice cream with warm Remus Lupin's Blood Substitute (see below).

Remus Lupin's Blood Substitute

Combine ½ cup corn syrup, 12 drops of red food coloring, and three drops of blue food coloring. Heat in a double boiler or microwave oven. Do not boil. Add a drop of almond extract, or the flavoring extract of your choice.

Domestic Eyeballs of Newts

Green or red grapes. Peeling the grapes is a nice touch and can be made less tedious by briefly dipping the grapes into boiling water.

Imported Eyeballs of Newt

Make lemon or white grape gelatin according to the package directions. Pour it into round ice cube trays. Refrigerate for 45 minutes. Place a blueberry in every sphere and press it to the bottom. Refrigerate two hours before unmolding and serving.

Chocolate Frogs

Melt chocolate chips in a double boiler or microwave oven. Pour the chocolate into frog molds (available in craft stores). Refrigerate until hard.

Sibyll Trelawney's Magical Divination Brew

Combine 2 liters of orange soda, a 46-ounce can of pineapple juice, and a 15-ounce can of condensed milk in a punch bowl. *Optional:* Float orange sherbet on top and/or add an ice ring or ice cubes made with pineapple juice, into which plastic spiders have been frozen.

Cold Butterbeer

By the glass: Combine eight ounces of chilled cream soda, two tablespoons butterscotch ice cream topping, and one small scoop of vanilla ice cream. Whisk to froth it.

By the bowl: Combine two liters (one large bottle) chilled cream soda, eight ounces butterscotch ice cream topping, and one pint of vanilla ice cream. Whisk the ice cream a bit to froth it.

Hot Butterbeer

By the mug: Combine one cup of milk and two tablespoons of butterscotch ice cream topping in a saucepan and gently warm it. Do not boil. Melt two ounces of marshmallow creme (or marshmallows) and one tablespoon of butter in a double boiler or microwave oven and stir until thoroughly mixed. Pour the butterscotch milk into a mug and top it with the marshmallow mixture.

By the quart: Follow the instructions for Hot Butterbeer by the mug, but use one quart of milk and ½ cup of butterscotch ice cream topping for the liquid. Top with a melted mixture of eight ounces of marshmallows or marshmallow creme and four tablespoons (½ stick) of butter.

Pumpkin Juice

Combine one 15-oz can of cooked pumpkin with ¾ cup sugar, one teaspoon cinnamon, ½ teaspoon ground ginger, and ¼ teaspoon ground cloves. For a single serving, mix ¼ cup of the spiced pumpkin mixture with one cup of apple cider. For a bowl of pumpkin juice, mix the entire 15 ounces of spiced pumpkin mixture with eight cups of apple cider. The pumpkin juice can be served over ice or heated gently and served warm in a mug.

Pumpkin Pasties

Make a boxed spice cake according to the package directions, but leave out the water and add 7½ ounces of canned pumpkin (half of a 15-ounce can). If you want flatter pasties, add a little water (about ¼ cup). Using a tablespoon, drop batter onto a greased baking sheet. Bake at 350° F for about 10 minutes. Remove from the oven, cool slightly on the cookie sheet, then cool completely on a wire rack.

Meanwhile, make a filling by combining the remaining pumpkin (7½ ounces) with ¼ teaspoon cinnamon, ⅛ teaspoon ground ginger, ⅛ teaspoon ground nutmeg, a pinch of ground cloves, ⅓ cup solid vegetable shortening, 5½ tablespoons butter, one cup confectioner's sugar, and one cup of marshmallow creme. Beat the mixture until smooth. Put a heaping tablespoon of filling on the bottom of one of the cakes. Put another cake on top of it to make a sandwich. Wrap it in waxed paper. Makes about 1 dozen pasties the size of small hamburgers.

Useful Web Sites

Because the Harry Potter series appeals so strongly to an adult audience, there are many good fan sites on the Internet. We believe the ones we have listed are appropriate for students old enough to read the books, but there are elements on some of the sites that are aimed at adult, rather than student, readers. We recommend that adults look at all Web sites before children access them, and that is especially true of Web sites devoted to the world of Harry Potter.

Harry Potter and the Wizard World:
The Harry Potter Lexicon, Steve Vander Ark
www.hp-lexicon.org/index-2.html
A compendium of Harry Potter information.

Harry Potter Guide, The Unofficial Guide to Harry Potter Fun, Facts and Trivia: Part 1
www.webrary.org/Kids/jharrypotter.html
A Web site listing characters, creatures, and settings in the Harry Potter series.

Harry Potter Guide, The Unofficial Guide to Harry Potter Fun, Facts and Trivia: Part 2
www.webrary.org/kids/jharrypotter2.html#food
Trivia, glossary, lists of foods and drink, and curses in the series.

Harry Potter, KidsFunOnline, Scholastic
www.scholastic.com/harrypotter/home.asp
Official Harry Potter Web site.

Hog's Head Kitchen, The Hog's Head
ciaran35.tripod.com/123/id41.html
Recipes for Treacle Fudge, Ton-tongue Toffee, and other treats.

J. K. Rowling Official Site
www.jkrowling.com/
The author's official Web site.

Quidditch.com
www.quidditch.com/index.html
Links to a variety of Hogwarts and Quidditch sites.

Wizard-world Money

Harry Potter Currency Converter, CNN Money
cgi.money.cnn.com/apps/hpcurrconv
A currency converter for U.S. money to wizard-world money.

Quidditch

Muggle Quidditch, Harry Potter and the Freakish Fans of Linlithgow
www.whitten.demon.co.uk/potter/mugglequidditch.htm
Quidditch rules.

Quidditch Standard Rules, Non-magical Rules Adapted for Ground Restricted Muggles
knology.net/~lionheart/Quidditch/Quidditch.html
Ground Quidditch rules.

Origami Animals

Enchanted Learning Software's Origami Jumping Frog, Enchanted Learning
www.enchantedlearning.com/crafts/origami/frog/
Origami version of Neville's toad, Trevor.

Night Owl Origami
www.maryannfraser.com/origami.htm
Instructions for Origami owls.

Books in the Series

Harry Potter and the Sorcerer's Stone

Harry Potter and the Chamber of Secrets

Harry Potter and the Prisoner of Azkaban

Harry Potter and the Goblet of Fire

Harry Potter and the Order of the Phoenix

Harry Potter and the Half-Blood Prince

Harry Potter Schoolbooks

Fantastic Beasts and Where to Find Them by Newt Scamander (a.k.a. J. K. Rowling)

Quidditch through the Ages by Kennilworthy Whisp (a.k.a. J. K. Rowling)

Artemis Fowl

Author: Eoin Colfer • **Publisher:** Hyperion Books • **Age Level:** 10 years old to young adult

In the first book of this Ireland-based series, 12-year-old genius Artemis Fowl, embittered by the disappearance of his father, decides to restore his family fortune by capturing a fairy and holding her for a ransom of fairy gold. Unfortunately for Artemis, he captures Captain Holly Short, a tough veteran of the LEPrecon (Lower Element Police Reconnaissance) Unit. In Book Two, Captain Short and her colleagues assist in the rescue of Artemis's father from the Russian underworld in return for Artemis's assistance in fighting off a takeover in the fairy world. In Book Three, a still-conniving Artemis attempts to use fairy technology to extort money from an American business magnate, then must turn to the fairy Lower Element Police to help undo the trouble he has unleashed.

The Artemis Fowl books have been described as "elves with an edge" and "Tom Clancy meets Harry Potter." Eoin Colfer himself describes the series as "DIE HARD with Fairies." The books are high-energy, high-tech thrillers that reinvent the world of fairies, trolls, and centaurs in a way that makes them appealing to older readers.

The use of codes and ciphers, the action-movie energy level, the colorful characters, and the young adult age level are all wonderfully compatible elements for an Artemis Fowl Ball.

Artemis Fowl Ball

Invitations

Encourage participants to create invitations, fliers, and/or posters announcing an Artemis Fowl costume dance. Information can be written in Gnommish or Centaurian as long as a translation key is available or some of the posters are written in Mud People language. (See the Gnommish Two-Way Translator and Eoin Colfer's Web site, listed on page 78, for translation keys.) Participants might also create a "Who's Who" of Artemis Fowl's world in order to assist those who haven't read the books in creating a costume.

Decorations

Recruit a committee to decorate the gym or hall where the dance will take place. One end of the room could be the world of Artemis Fowl (rooms in the Fowl family mansion, where objects are embellished with the family motto, Aurum est Potestas/Gold is Power). The other end of the hall could look like the fairy lower element (cave backdrops of dark cardboard or cloth with aluminum foil diamonds that would glitter when they catch the light) or the green Irish woods of Tara 1. A disco ball hung from the ceiling would add the effect of flying fairies to the room.

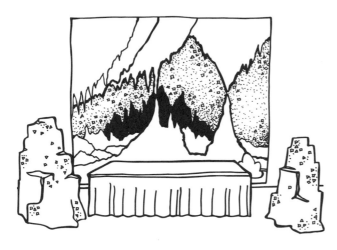

Music

The Lower Element would probably prefer the simple tunes of old Ireland, especially those that mention fairies, elves, and little people. Enlist the services of a fiddler and someone who can demonstrate an Irish jig.

On the other hand, Artemis Fowl is a high-tech boy who would probably prefer electronic music. Some possibilities include songs by Basement Jaxx, Chemical Brothers, Crystal Method, dj tiestro, Infected Mushroom, Juno Reactor, and The Prodigy. Members of the Artemis Fowl Ball planning committee could probably come up with a long list of CDs to play.

Irish and electronic music could alternate or eventually escalate into a battle between Lower Element and Mud People bands.

Evoke the luminescent glow of the Lower Element tunnels by ending the evening with glow stick dancing. Encourage participants to bring their own glow sticks or provide, free of charge or for a small price, glow sticks and glow necklaces. (Glow products can be bought in bulk at party stores or online. See page 78 for advice on glow stick selection from Glowsticking.com.) Turn down the lights, turn up the music, and let the Artemis Fowl Ball come to a phosphorescent finale.

Refreshment Tables

Artemis Fowl's Food Table

Cover a long table with a white linen tablecloth or a paper tablecloth that looks like lace or linen. Place a candelabra in the middle of the table, on top of a cardboard place mat with the Fowl family crest (Aurum est Potestas). Set the table with gold plates (or plastic plates covered with gold foil). Serve golden foods, such as golden trail mix (made with golden cereal, nuts, and golden raisins), cheese and crackers, yellow cake with gold-colored frosting and gold coin decorations, and Rice Krispies® bars wrapped in gold foil to look like bars of gold bullion. For beverages, serve golden punch or tea punch.

The Lower Element Food Table

Cover a table with a length of metallic tulle fabric, plastic jewels, and a variety of polished or unpolished rocks. Serve vegetables, carrot cake (for Foaly the Centaur), rock candy, and Mulch Diggums cake. For beverages, offer bottled spring water or orange plasma punch.

Recipes

Mulch Diggums Soil Strata Cake

- 1 box chocolate cake mix
- 2 boxes instant pudding, both chocolate, or 1 chocolate and 1 butterscotch, vanilla, or pistachio
- 1 can vanilla frosting *(optional)*
- vanilla wafers, or graham crackers *(optional)*
- coconut *(optional)*
- gummy worms and rock candy *(optional)*

Prepare a two-layer boxed chocolate cake and instant pudding according to the package directions. When the cake layers are cool, fill a pastry tube or baster with the chocolate pudding. Insert the nozzle of the pastry tube into the bottom layer of the cake and inject some of the pudding. Repeat in several areas of the cake.

Spread the top of the first cake layer with more chocolate pudding, or with butterscotch pudding, vanilla pudding, or frosting to which a drop of yellow food coloring has been added. Top with the second layer of the cake. Use the pastry tube to inject the top layer with chocolate pudding. Frost the top of the cake with pudding or with frosting. To make the top of the cake look like sand, add a drop of yellow food coloring to vanilla pudding or frosting, then sprinkle finely crumbled graham crackers or vanilla wafers on top of the iced cake. To make the top of the cake look like grass, use pistachio pudding or vanilla frosting to which green food coloring has been added. Tint coconut with green food coloring and sprinkle on top of the iced cake.

Decorate the cake with rock candy crystals and gummy worms.

Rock Candy

Bring 1½ cups of water to a boil in a saucepan. Remove from heat and add three cups of sugar, stirring well to dissolve. Slowly add three more cups of sugar, re-heating the liquid if necessary to coax the sugar to dissolve. When the sugar is completely dissolved, pour the liquid into three heat-proof glass jars. Tie three 6" lengths of string to three pencils and lay the pencils over the openings of the jars so that the strings hang down into the sugar water. Crystals will start to form along the string within an hour and will continue to form for several days. If a layer of sugar forms on the surface of the liquid, break it. When the water evaporates, the candy is done.

Artemis Fowl's Golden Punch

Put ½ gallon pineapple or lemon sherbet into a punch bowl. Add two quarts of golden ginger ale or one quart ginger ale and one quart yellow lemonade. For decoration, float a coin-filled ice ring in the punch.

To make the ice ring, place gold foil-wrapped chocolate coins in the bottom of a gelatin mold or bundt cake pan. Pour ginger ale into the mold to the desired depth of the mold. To distribute the coins through the ring, put some of the coins in the bottom of the mold and cover with one or two inches of ginger ale. Freeze, then add more coins and another inch or two of ginger ale. Return to the freezer. Continue until the ring is frozen to the desired depth.

Artemis Fowl's Tea Punch

Combine two cups strongly brewed tea, six cups pineapple or orange juice, and two cups ginger ale. Add simple syrup to taste. Float an ice block of foil-wrapped chocolate coins in the punch to keep it cool.

Simple Syrup

Combine two cups of sugar and one cup of water in a saucepan. Warm over low heat until the sugar is dissolved. Increase the heat and boil for one minute. Store in a clear glass jar. In addition to the tea punch, use simple syrup to sweeten iced tea and lemonade.

Coin-filled Ice Block

To scatter coins evenly through the block of ice, put a few foil-covered chocolate coins on the bottom of an empty, clean milk container from which the top has been cut away. Cover with an inch or two of ginger ale, tea, or pineapple juice. Freeze. Add a few more coins and another inch or two of liquid. Continue the process until the entire cube is frozen. To position some of the coins vertically rather than horizontally, partially freeze a layer, and carefully slip the coins into the ice matrix so that they are standing on their edges. Return the mold to the freezer until the block is frozen solid.

Orange Plasma Punch

Put ½ gallon orange sherbet into a punch bowl. Add two quarts of golden ginger ale, or one quart of ginger ale and one quart of orange juice. Freeze a ring of ginger ale or orange juice in a gelatin mold and float it in the punch to keep it cold. Give the concoction a Lower Element phosphorescent glow by dropping a washed, lighted glow stick into the punch and holding it under the surface with the frozen ring.

Costumes

Encourage guests to get into the spirit of the Artemis Fowl books by attending the Artemis Fowl Ball dressed as one of their favorite characters.

Holly Short, Commander Root, and other fairies in LEPrecon wear black jumpsuits decorated with LEPrecon shields and badges. Weapons and gadgets include wrist computers, fairy locators, mesmers, fairy sonix grenades, Koboi DoubleDex wings, antiradiation suits and spray, buzz batons and moonbelts. Fairies and elves have pointy ears.

Trolls and dwarfs like Mulch Diggums, wear loose, sloppy clothes in shades of brown and gray, often smeared with food stains. Mulch Diggums looks like a warthog.

Artemis Fowl and Butler are always impeccably attired in suits and ties. Juliet Butler dresses in a feminine manner, but is almost as precise as her brother. All three have night vision goggles and sunglasses to resist mind wipe technology. Artemis has the C cube, and Juliet has a jade ring braided into her hair.

Fairy Wing Franchise

Consider making a quantity of Fairy Wings for sale the night of the Artemis Fowl Ball. Ask local supermarkets for cardboard boxes. Assemble a crew of wing workers, including someone reliable enough to handle a box cutter safely. Follow the directions below for Quick and Easy Koboi DoubleDex Wings. Experiment with a variety of colors, surfaces, and effects. On the night of the Artemis Fowl Ball, hang the wings from a coat stand at a "Wings for Sale" table. Enlist a volunteer to sell the wings or put out a money jar and use the honor system. Alternatively, hang the wings on a coat stand and encourage guests to take and return them at will and without charge.

Quick and Easy Koboi DoubleDex Fairy Wings: Start with a cardboard box, ideally one that is more rectangular than square. Using a box cutter, cut off all of the flaps on the top and bottom of the box. Cut off one of the short sides of the box and lay the three remaining sides flat on the cutting surface. Using several layers of cardboard to protect the cutting surface from damage, use the box cutter to shape the two long sides of the box to look like fairy wings. Trim the middle section (which will fit along the wearer's back) so that it is a bit shorter than the wings from top to bottom. Decorate the cardboard wings by painting both sides with a combination of tempera paint, glitter glue, or glitter fabric paint. Or use white glue to attach aluminum foil, metallic tulle fabric, or scales made from glossy magazine pages to both sides of the wings. With the end of a pen or screwdriver, make two holes, in a vertical line but several inches apart, on each side of the middle section of the wings. Run a 40" length of ribbon or cord through the two holes and tie the ends together, creating a loop large enough to slip over the wearer's shoulders. Knot the ribbon loosely so the wearer can untie it and readjust the wings to his or her size.

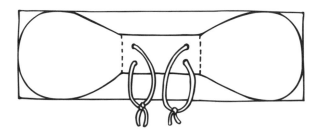

Other Activities

Enlist a volunteer to film an Iriscam report of the ball for later study by Foaly at LEP HQ. Pay particularly close attention to Mulch Diggums, who can't be trusted, and to Artemis Fowl, who can't be trusted, either.

Enlist student or adult volunteers to record the ball with digital cameras. A little creative work on the computer might yield interesting photos of the principal with a troll on his head, or other evidence of Mud People and the denizens of the Lower Element partying together. Post the photos on the school or library's Web site, or print the photos, create labels, and display them in the school or library's lobby.

Web Sites

Eoin Colfer's Web Site
homepage.eircom.net/~eoincolfer65/home.htm
Short biography of the author and a link to the code page for substitution codes used in the books.

Gnommish Two-Way Translator
www.stolaf.edu/people/hansonr/translate/gnommish/gnommish.htm
A translator page for the gnommish code in Book One.

Guide to Glowsticks, BigUglyFly
www.glowsticking.com/nu/item/24/catid/9
Advice about dancing with and purchasing glowsticks, including recommendations for online sources.

Penguin Books' Artemis Fowl Web Site
www.artemisfowl.co.uk/
Biographies of the author and characters in the books, a message board, games, and contests.

The World of Eoin Colfer's Artemis Fowl Stories
www.bbc.co.uk/dna/h2g2/A994791
A BBC community Web site with an overview of the major characters.

Books in the Series

Artemis Fowl

Artemis Fowl: The Arctic Incident

Artemis Fowl: The Eternity Code

Artemis Fowl: The Opal Deception

Artemis Fowl: The Seventh Dwarf (A 60-page mini-novel in which the action takes place between Book One and Book Two of the Artemis Fowl series.)

The Artemis Fowl Files